Looking at the U.S. White Working Class Historically

David Gilbert

D0104445

2017

Looking at the U.S. White Working Class Historically
by David Gilbert

copyright David Gilbert, 2017

this edition copyright Kersplebedeb

ISBN: 978-1-894946-91-9

Kersplebedeb Publishing and Distribution
CP 63560
CCCP Van Horne
Montreal, Quebec
Canada H3W 3H8

www.kersplebedeb.com
www.leftwingbooks.net

Printed in Canada

Contents

Preface to the 1984 Edition

One of the supreme issues for our movement is summed-up in the contradictions of the term "white working class." On one hand there is the class designation that should imply, along with all other workers of the world, a fundamental role in the overthrow of capitalism. On the other hand, there is the identification of being part of a ("white") oppressor nation.

Historically, we must admit that the identity with the oppressor nation has been primary. There have been times of fierce struggle around economic issues but precious little in the way of a revolutionary challenge to the system itself. There have been moments of uniting with Black and other Third World workers in union struggles, but more often than not an opposition to full equality and a disrespect for the self-determination of other oppressed peoples. These negative trends have been particularly pronounced within the current era of history (since World War II). White labor has been either a legal opposition within or an active component of the U.S. imperial system.

There have been two basic responses to this reality by the white Left. (1) The main position by far has been opportunism. This has entailed an unwillingness to recognize the leading role within the U.S. of national liberation struggles, a failure to make the fight against white supremacy a conscious and prime element of all organizing, and, related to the above, a general lack of revolutionary combativeness against the imperial state. More specifically, opportunism either justifies the generally racist history of the white working class and our Left or romanticizes that history by presenting it as much more anti-racist than reality merits. (2) Our own tendency, at its best moments, has recognized the leading role of national liberation and the essential position of solidarity to building any revolutionary consciousness among whites. We have often, however, fallen into an elitist or perhaps defeatist view that dismisses the possibility of organizing significant numbers of white people, particularly working-class whites.

There is very little analysis, and even less practice, that is both real about the nature and consciousness of the white working class and yet holds out the prospect of organizing a large number on a revolutionary basis. This fissure will not be joined by some magical leap of abstract thought—either by evoking classical theories of class or by lapsing into cultural or biological determinism. We must use our tools of analysis (materialism) to understand concretely how this contradiction developed (historically). But an historical view cannot be static. In seeing how certain forces developed, we must also look (dialectically) at under what conditions and through what means the contradiction can be transformed.

Introduction to the 2017 Edition

The main purpose of my writing from prison is to contribute what I can to developing effective movements against imperialism. "Imperialism" is, I think, the best brief way to name the prevailing system, which encompasses a range of oppressions and horrors: a global economy that condemns billions of human beings to abject poverty; the wars, coups, assassinations, manipulations used to enforce that; the patriarchy that not only attacks and restricts the lives of half of humankind and generates vicious homo- and transphobia, but that also diminishes the humanity of all of us; the stark class divisions and exploitation; the countless ways, such as ableism, that people are demeaned and limited; the rapacious and hyper-wasteful global economy that is rapidly destroying the earth as a habitat for humanity.

"Looking at the White Working Class Historically" has been the piece of my writing that younger-generations activists, especially white anti-racists, have found most helpful. That response provided the impetus to write a new section, about the past forty-five years, which has been added on to produce this new edition. We changed the title a bit from the earlier edition to be clear that we are discussing only the white working class within the U.S., without any specific examination of the many other white working classes in Europe and in various settler colonies around the world, which have overlapping but varied histories. At the same time that "Looking…" has been my most useful writing, it is deeply flawed in a number of ways. Ideally, I would do a lot more study and re-write the entire text. As a thin gruel substitute for that desired hearty meal, I'll spotlight some of those concerns in this introduction, below. First I want to take a moment to talk about how the text evolved.

"Looking…" was not conceived as a single essay. Rather, the different sections were written as I came across the relevant readings or dialogs, sometimes separated by years, and now decades. The journey began in jail in Rockland County, New York, as part of the many political discussions with my co-defendants and comrades (ex-Black Panthers) Kuwasi Balagoon and Sekou Odinga. At that time, someone sent me Ted Allen's "White Supremacy." A year or so later, upstate at Auburn prison, I finally read W.E.B. DuBois's seminal and essential *Black Reconstruction*, about the pivotal period of the Civil War and its aftermath. A little while after that I received J. Sakai's *Settlers*, with its laser beam illumination across the scope of U.S. history.

Initially each section was done separately, as a review of the particular work as I read it. Then they were put together in 1984. When Cooperative Distribution Service proposed re-issuing the pamphlet in 1991, J. Sakai urged me to write what became the fourth section, "Some Lessons From the Sixties." We also included Sakai's response to how I had defined the position of white workers somewhat differently from *Settlers*—without our trying to resolve it into a pat conclusion. Of course, by 1991 we were already well past the 1960s and into a new stage. In the 1990s, I wrote elsewhere about growing white worker frustrations and the intensifying politics of racial scapegoating, but I didn't take that on as a needed fifth section until now.

Serious flaws resulted from my sticking too closely to the limits of the texts being reviewed, especially Ted Allen's, which makes the crucial white/Black access into the whole story. I did say, "[...] it is a problem that he doesn't analyze the other major foundation of white supremacy: the theft of Native lands through genocide." Also, where Allen extols Bacon's Rebellion as whites and Blacks fighting side by side, I disagreed, pointing out that "Bacon's cause was to exterminate the Indians." But those qualifiers weren't nearly strong enough. Allen's silence about the genocidal wars on the Indigenous populations means his analysis, while having some valid points, is fundamentally flawed. While I can't provide an adequate presentation, I highly recommend Roxanne Dunbar-Ortiz's *An Indigenous Peoples' History of the United States* (2014) as an absolute must-read for understanding U.S. history. In addition, Allen glosses over the differences from the beginning between white indentured servants brought here under onerous contracts and Africans hunted down and shipped over in chains.

The response to the 1991 edition showed me that some people like the Allen analysis because they see it as centering the rise of white supremacy solely in what happened on those Virginia plantations in the 17th century. If it were *only* that, racism would be a lot easier to overcome than reality permits. Let's be clear: we do not further working-class organizing by pretending that the obstacles are superficial or simple. Allen's tunnel vision on the

Virginia plantations extracts them from the framework of global conquest and exploitation and thereby misses how they were a particular development within a much broader and much deeper history. Racism was already rampant based on the white supremacist structures of the invasions of the Americas; the enslavement of Indigenous nations, most massively with the concentrated populations in South America; the trans-Atlantic slave trade that led to the capturing, killing, and enslaving of over 100 million Africans; the highly lucrative plantations in the Caribbean; and more. My review was seriously flawed in failing to state that these white supremacist tectonic plates are the underlying basis for the destructive and continuing earthquakes of racism. It would be a serious mistake to take Allen's account as the sole, or even main, story. With that being said, I still find his pamphlet very helpful in highlighting the role and potential of servile rebellions and in showing how the ruling class response was to draw sectors of white labor further into the structures of white supremacy in order to use them as shock troops to suppress Black resistance—and, we must add, to steal Native lands.[1]

My pamphlet also failed to integrate these realities with the preceding basis in patriarchy. I still don't know enough to fill in that history; Maria Mies's *Patriarchy and Accumulation on a World Scale* (1986) provides a sharp analysis of the parallels between patriarchy and colonialism and their ongoing roles in the raking in of capitalist profits. Here I'll just note that it's not purely coincidental that a Europe that burned tens of thousands of "witches" in the interest of subordinating women also carried out the satanic looting of the Americas, the horrendous trans-Atlantic slave trade, the ruthless plunder of India, and the destructive drive to dominate nature. Another place where my politics on women fell short is my discussion (p. 45) of the early 1970s divergence between the anti-imperialist and women's liberation movements. I should have noted and stressed that women of color had begun to fight on multiple fronts, against sexism, racism, and imperialism, which would show the way out of this divide. By the late 1970s the women of color movement articulated a principled politics, now usually referred to as the intersectionality of oppressions and resistance. Another weakness was that my discussion of the 20th century did not emphasize enough imperialism's super-exploitation of the Third World (the Global South) and the way some of those profits are used to buy off large sectors of the working class at home.

When these writings began, my politics had been shaped by the high tide of national liberation struggles and the hope that they were leading the way to world revolution. Similarly, within the U.S., revolutionary nationalism was the predominant politics of radical people of color. Black people, Indigenous nations, Puerto Ricans, and Chicanos were all fighting for self-determination and then to reclaim and redirect their economies to meet people's needs. Militant Asian American groups fighting racism also demanded self-determination. In that context, the term "white working class" indicated the working class of a separate, oppressor nation. As Sakai points out in *Settlers*, much of the most exploited labor was done by a "colonial proletariat" made up of workers from those various internal oppressed nations.

The terms are not as clear cut today. Revolutionary nationalism is still a valid and vital position, and self-determination a basic demand. But there is more variety in how people interact, in forms of struggle, and in ultimate vision. It's not up to me to try to define how these questions will be resolved. I haven't made changes in my earlier wording nor worried if my terminology is a bit different today. I did add a clarification, to be more explicit, that the white working class is not the whole U.S. working class. Also, that U.S. working class has changed considerably over the years, now involving a lot more women as well as immigrants from many more countries. As always, much of the most arduous and exploited labor is done by a now wider range of people of color.

Whether or not the U.S. ultimately breaks up into different nations, the challenge for white radicals, to whom this book is primarily addressed, is how to be principled allies to people of color struggles, how to implement accountability to them, how to successfully organize significant numbers of white people on an anti-racist basis.

The post-1971 section was long overdue when I finally started writing in 2015. I was making slow progress when the Trump campaign erupted, a new crescendo in the politics of racial scapegoating. Among the host of more dire consequences, I felt annoyed that my writing switched from illuminating trends to falling in their shadow. And I certainly couldn't see how my voice could be heard and my positions differentiated amid the roar of the storm of Left commentaries. So when my friend Ken Yale urged me to write an introduction about the Trump phenomenon, I balked...but finally he prevailed. Here I've moved those five pages on Trump up to become the opening for the whole book. That change has the advantage of making "Looking..." more engaged with current struggles, but runs the risk of soon becoming dated. The centuries-long history of white supremacy will always be fundamental to political challenges and tasks as long as imperialism survives.

The loud thunderclap of Trump's shocking win set off an avalanche of analysis. Some liberals laid this travesty at the feet of the racism of the white working class, a convenient deflection from how the Democratic Party stood for global capitalism and the frustrations it engenders. Labor-oriented Leftists sharply counterattacked against this blaming of the working class, but often in ways that papered over the problem of racism. One example is a statistic I've seen cited about a dozen different times. Using income as a convenient if very rough indication of class, these articles highlight how exit polls showed that the majority of those making less than $50,000 a year voted for Hillary Clinton; the tally for those making less than $30,000 went even a bit more her way.

That often-cited proof is a statistical sleight of hand that turns reality, in terms of white working people's consciousness, upside down. As these commentators should know, the lower the income level the higher the proportion of people of color—who overwhelmingly voted against Trump. For voting statistics to be a meaningful tool of analysis, we have to look at both class and race.

Among *all* voters making less than $30,000 a year, 53% voted for Clinton and 41% for Trump. For *white* voters at that income level, it was 34% for Clinton and 58% for

Trump.[2] We can't meet the challenges ahead by touting grossly misleading statistics. Instead, we need to face the reality that among working-class whites who voted the majority went for the billionaire demagogue who spearheaded his campaign with racial scapegoating.

Blaming the working class is a misdirection; but so too is denialism about the depth and penetration of white supremacy, which has been the basis for the white Left's failures over the past 150 years. Our only chance for success is to grapple with the reality and then work to develop programs and approaches that can achieve some breakthroughs. While I toss out some suggestions in this book, I expect we'll learn a lot more from the conscious work, then evaluations, and then new efforts of the several activist groups that are now trying to organize in a principled way. My fondest hope for "Looking…" is that it can provide some background helpful to those honestly facing the challenge of organizing large numbers of working-class whites against racism and for their long term interests and needs for a cooperative, creative, sustainable and loving world.

The Context for the Trump Phenomenon (2017)

The bizarre and dangerous rise of Donald Trump did not just pop up out of thin air. The very foundation of the U.S. is white supremacy. This country is, at its core, imperialist, patriarchal, and based in a range of ways human beings are delimited and demeaned. Nor are the specific and terribly virulent politics of racial scapegoating brand new. Always a part of U.S. culture, that approach became more central in mainstream politics, with various ups and downs in the rhetoric, since the end of the 1960s. A stable imperialism prefers to rule by keeping the population passive, with large sectors at home placated by relative prosperity. But when the system is in crisis, those running the economy often resort to diverting anger by scapegoating the racial "other." The sectors of the population who buy into that get the "satisfaction" of stomping on their "inferiors," which is a lot easier than confronting the mega-powerful ruling class.

The eruption of mass protest against Trump has been exciting, and so far it has been sustained. People seem to have a feel for the critical need for ongoing education, organizing, and mobilization. The movement also has to be prepared, both psychologically and in terms of legal and support networks, for greater repression, both state and extralegal.

The Democrats, in blaming "those damn Russkies," are deflecting attention away from the real reason they lost: they represented the prevailing global capitalism and all the associated frustrations of the decline of U.S. manufacturing and the erosion of job security. Trump spoke to those anxieties—in a totally demagogic and dishonest way. For example, during the campaign he railed against Goldman Sachs as the prime example of how Wall Street banks screw the working man; then, as president he selected seven of his top economic appointments from the ranks of Goldman Sachs. The Democrats could not provide a compelling alternative to this racist scam artist because they too are deeply rooted in the long bipartisan history of white supremacy, capitalism, and wars of aggression.

Regardless of these questionable charges, Russia can't hold a candle to the U.S. when it comes to interfering in other countries' elections, let alone more intrusive and violent means of regime change. The big push by the Democrats and allied sectors of the security apparatus for confronting Russia is not only unjustified but also runs the risk of leading to a horribly destructive war. As much as we're scandalized, and rightly so, by Trump's more blatant racism and misogyny, we need to look at the continuities as well as the departures.

President Obama, with his kinder and more inclusive rhetoric, provided trillions of dollars to bail out Wall Street at the expense of Main Street. He presided over seven wars (drone strikes have killed hundreds of civilians and are acts of war under international law). His administration deported a record number of immigrants. In his last year, Obama sought to burnish his legacy around climate change and mass incarceration. He brought his eight-year total of clemencies up to 1,715, the most since President Truman, but earlier took legal action to keep far more in prison. After Congress passed a law somewhat reducing what had been incredibly harsh sentences for crack cocaine, the Justice Department went to court to prevent any retroactive application, and thus kept some 6,000 people behind bars. Similarly, Obama issued a number of executive orders, most of which can be readily reversed, to modestly rein in greenhouse gases. But earlier his administration played a key role in sabotaging the 2009 Copenhagen Conference of Parties, which was the best chance to get a binding international treaty with some teeth in it, at a time when Democrats held a majority in Congress.

Recalling these dire problems is a reminder of how much the most basic issue is the very nature of the system. Nonetheless, there is something new and particularly threatening about Trump's election: the way he has enlarged, energized, and emboldened an active and aggressive base for white supremacy. Immigrants, Muslims, Native American water protectors, Black Lives Matter activists, women who've faced sexual assault, LGBTQ folks, those who can't afford health insurance, and more all feel under the gun. The prospect of an unbridled pouring of more greenhouse gases into the atmosphere is terrifying. And there is a great danger he could provoke a major war, since in the past that has been the most effective way for unpopular presidents to rally public support behind them. We need much more of an anti-war movement.

We can't forget that an imperialism in crisis will turn to racist mobilizations to supersede obstacles to continued domination and expansion. Racist mass mobilizations constitute a central force for building fascism.[3] Even if the U.S. isn't fully there yet, the 2016 election moved us farther down that fraught road. To deal with this historic challenge we have to understand that the basis is the decline of imperialism. The U.S., while still the predominant power, has been teetering in and out of economic and political crises since 1971. And on top of that, we now are on the brink of environmental disasters that can't be resolved under capitalism.

As of this writing (February 2017) major sectors of the ruling class are still wary of Trump, seeing him as too much of a loose cannon. They are making an effort to at least rein him in if not bring him down, although leading with the very dangerous push toward greater confrontation with Russia. It remains to be seen if Trump's amalgam of billionaire businessmen and ultra-Right white nationalists can provide a coherent program or even hold together. Whatever happens with his presidency, we likely are in for a burgeoning of white supremacist movements. If Trump's economic policies appear to be successful (possible in the short run of a couple of years but, if so, with giant dislocations and problems in the longer run), he's a hero to those embittered sectors of the white working and middle classes who voted for him. On the other hand, if his administration implodes, millions of his fervent supporters will see it as the "elites" bringing down their champion. In either case our job, our challenge, is to build a strong movement that can articulate the real issues and clearly present humane, international, and sustainable alternatives.

There's been an outpouring of Left analysis on who voted for Trump and why. Some of it is very helpful about race, class, and the economy. From what I've seen there hasn't been enough about how the U.S., from the very beginning, was built on the foundation of white supremacy and patriarchy. There's been very little that puts all that in the global context, with the U.S. as the premier imperial power but in decline. Nor has there been enough that has rooted Trump's rise in the developments of the past forty-five years. This is the challenge for our ongoing project of analysis and activism.

Looking at the U.S.
White Working Class Historically (1984)

In this review, I want to look at three historical studies that contribute to the needed discussion: *(1)* Ted Allen's two essays in *White Supremacy* (a collection printed by Sojourner Truth Organization); *(2)* W.E.B. DuBois, *Black Reconstruction* (New York: 1933); *(3)* J. Sakai, *Settlers: The Mythology of the White Proletariat* (Chicago: 1983).*[Editor's note: The page references for Settlers in the discussion that follows have been updated to correspond with the more recent 2014 edition.]*

1. White Supremacy In the U.S.; Slavery and the Origins Of Racism (Ted Allen)

Allen's two essays provide us with a very cogent and useful account of the development of the structure of white supremacy in the U.S. He shows both how this system was consciously constructed by the colonial ("Plantation Bourgeoisie") ruling class and what was the initial impact on the development of the white laborers. Contrary to the cynical view that racism is a basic to human nature and that there always has been (and therefore always will be) a fundamental racial antagonism, Allen shows that systematic white supremacy developed in a particular historical period, for specific material reasons.

> "Up to the 1680s little distinction was made in the status of Blacks and English and other Europeans held in involuntary servitude. Contrary to common belief the status of Blacks in the first seventy years of Virginia colony was not that of racial, lifelong, hereditary slavery, and the majority of the whites who came were not 'free'. Black and white servants intermarried, escaped together, and rebelled together." (p. 3)

A rapidly developing plantation system required an expanding labor supply. The solution was both to have more servants and to employ them for longer terms. A move from fixed-term servitude (e.g., seven years) to perpetual slavery would be valuable to the ruling class of the new plantation economy. The question for analysis is not so much why there was a transition to chattel slavery but why it was not imposed on the white servants as well as on the Blacks. To analyze this development we need to understand that any method of exploiting labor requires a system of social control.

There were a series of servile rebellions that threatened the plantation system in the period preceding the transition to racially designated chattel slavery and white supremacy. Allen cites numerous examples. In 1661, Black and Irish servants joined in an insurrectionary plot in Bermuda. In 1663, in Virginia, there was an insurrection for the common freedom of Blacks, whites, and Indian servants. In the next twenty years, there were no fewer than ten popular and servile revolts and plots in Virginia. Also, many Black and white servants successfully escaped (to Indian territories) and established free societies.

Allen places particular emphasis on Bacon's rebellion which began in April 1676. This was a struggle within the ruling class over "Indian policy," but Bacon resorted to arming white and Black servants, promising them freedom. Allen says "the transcendent importance" of this revolt is that "the armed working class, Black and white, fought side by side for the abolition of slavery." He mentions, but doesn't deal with the reality, that Bacon's cause was to exterminate the Indians. Allen's focus is on the formation of chattel slavery, but it is a problem that he doesn't analyze the other major foundation of white supremacy:

the theft of Native lands through genocide.

The twenty-year period of servile rebellions made the issue of social control urgent for the plantation bourgeoisie, at the same time as they economically needed to move to a system of perpetual slavery. The purpose of creating a basic white/Black division was in order to have one section of labor police and control the other. As Allen says, *"The non-slavery of white labor was the indispensable condition for the slavery of black labor."*[4]

A series of laws were passed and practices imposed that forged a qualitative distinction between white and Black labor. In 1661 a Virginia law imposed twice the penalty time for escaped English bond-servants who ran away in the company of an African life-time bond-servant. Heavy penalties were imposed on white women servants who bore children fathered by Africans. One of the very first white servant privileges was the exemption of white servant women from work in the fields and the requirements through taxes to force Black children to go to work at twelve, while white servant children were excused until they were fourteen. In 1680, Negroes were forbidden to carry arms, defensive or offensive. At the same time, it was made legal to kill a Negro fugitive bond-servant who resisted recapture.

What followed 1680 was a twenty-five-year period of laws that systematically drew the color line as the limit on various economic, social, and political rights. By 1705, "the distinctions between white servants and Black slavery were fixed: Black slaves were to be held in life long hereditary slavery and whites for five years, with many rights and protections afforded to them by law." (p. 6)

19

We can infer from these series of laws that white laborers were not "innately racist" before the material and social distinctions were drawn. This is evidenced by the rulers' need to impose very harsh penalties against white servants who escaped with Blacks or who bore them children. As historian Philip Bruce observed of this period, many white servants "...had only recently arrived from England, and were therefore comparatively free from...race prejudice."

The white bond-servants now could achieve freedom after five years service: the white women and children, at least, were freed from the most arduous labor. The white bond-servant, once freed, had the prospect of the right to vote and to own land (at the Indians' expense).

These privileges did not come from the kindness of the planters' hearts nor from some form of racial solidarity. (Scottish coal miners were held in slavery in the same period of time.) Quite simply, the poor whites were needed and used as a force to suppress the main labor force: the African chattel slaves. The poor white men constituted the rank and file of the militias and later (beginning in 1727) the slave patrols. They were given added benefits, such as tax exemptions, to do so. By 1705, after Blacks had been stripped of the legal right to self-defense, the white bond-servant was given a musket upon completion of servitude. There was such a clear and conscious strategy that by 1698 there were even "deficiency laws" that required the plantation owners to maintain a certain ratio of white to African servants. The English Parliament, in 1717, passed a law making transportation to bond-servitude in the plantation colonies a legal punishment for crime. Another example of this conscious design is revealed in the Council of Trade and Plantation report to the king in 1721, saying that in South Carolina, "Black slaves have lately attempted and were very nearly succeeding in a new revolution—and therefore, it may be necessary to propose some new law for encouraging the entertainment of more white servants in the future."

It would be important to have a concomitant analysis of the role of the theft of Indian land and of the impact of the slave trade itself. Allen's analysis[5] of early plantation labor, however, provides an invaluable service.

When Black and white labor were in the same conditions of servitude, there was a good deal of solidarity. A system of white supremacy was consciously constructed in order to (1) extend and intensify exploitation (through chattel slavery) and (2) have shock troops (poor, but now privileged, whites) to suppress slave rebellions. Thus the 1680–1705 period[6] is a critical benchmark essential to understanding all subsequent North American history. As Allen tells us, "It was the bourgeoisie's deliberately contrived policy of differentiation between white and Black labor through the system of white skin privileges for white labor that allowed the bourgeoisie to use the poor whites as an instrument of social control over the Black workers." (p. 5)

Allen refers to, but doesn't fully develop, the impact of white supremacy on the white laborers. His general analysis is that by strengthening capitalist rule it reinforced exploitation of whites too: "... white supremacy [was] the keystone of capitalist rule which left white labor poor, exploited and increasingly powerless with respect to their rulers and exploiters." But since "the mass of poor whites was alienated from the black proletariat and enlisted as enforcers of bourgeois power" (p. 40), it would be useful to have more analysis of the interplay of these two contradictory roles: exploited/enforcers. In any case, the overall effect was to break the white workers from their proletarian class struggle alongside Blacks and to bind them more tightly to their own ruling class.

2. Black Reconstruction 1860–1880 (W.E.B. DuBois)

DuBois's work is a classic study, an absolutely essential reading to understanding U.S. history. The book deals not only with the Reconstruction period that followed the Civil War but also with the War itself and the period of slavery preceding it. This review will only focus on the insights about the relationship of white labor to Black people and their struggles. There are, however, two essential theses that DuBois puts forward that should be pointed out here.

(1) The slaves were not freed by Lincoln's or by the Union's benevolence. The slaves essentially freed themselves. First, they fled the plantations in great numbers, depleting the South of labor for its wartime economy. Secondly, they volunteered to fight with the Union to defeat the slavocracies. The Emancipation Proclamation of 1863 came only when Lincoln realized that he needed to use Black troops in order to win the war. (It applied only to states at war with the Union). Two hundred thousand Black troops made the decisive difference in the war.

(2) Reconstruction was not this period of unbridled corruption and of heartless oppression of the noble (white) South that has since been depicted by the propaganda of

history. Not only did Reconstruction see the active role of Black people in the government, but also, based on that, it was an era of democratic reform that brought such things as free public education, public works, and advances in women's rights to the South. At the same time, DuBois shows how Reconstruction was defeated by a systematic campaign of terror, with the complicity of the capitalist North.

DuBois's analysis of the pre-war South, starts with the basic structures (whose origins Allen described) in place and well developed. The system of slavery demanded a special police force and such a force was made possible and unusually effective by the presence of poor whites. By this time there were "more white people to police the slaves than there were slaves." (p. 12)

Still, there were very important class differentiations within the white population. 7% of the total white Southern population owned three quarters of the slaves. 70% owned no slaves at all. To DuBois, a basic issue is why the poor whites would agree to police the slaves. Since slavery competed with and thereby undercut the wages of white labor in the North, wouldn't it seem natural for poor whites in general to oppose slavery?

DuBois presents two main reasons: (1) Poor whites were provided with non-laboring jobs as overseers, slave-drivers, members of slave patrols. (DuBois doesn't indicate what percentage of whites held jobs like this). (2) There was the "vanity" of feeling associated with the master and the dislike of "negro" toil. The poor white never considered himself a laborer, rather he aspired to himself own slaves. These aspirations were not without some basis. (About one quarter of the Southern white population were petty bourgeois, small slave-owners).

> "The result was that the system was held stable and intact by the poor white … Gradually the whole white South became an armed and commissioned camp to keep Negroes in slavery and to kill the black rebel." (p. 12)

There was another factor that had a heavy impact on both poor whites in the South and the Northern working class. In early America, land was free (based on genocide of the Indians) and thus acquiring property was a possibility for nearly every thrifty worker. This access to property not only created a new petty bourgeoisie emerging out of the white working class, it also created an ideology of individual advancement rather than collective class struggle as the answer to exploitation.

The Northern working class tended to oppose the *spread* of slavery but not oppose slavery itself. If slavery came to the North it would compete with and undercut free labor. If the plantation system spread to the West, it would monopolize the land that white workers aspired to settle as small farmers. But there was very little pro-abolition sentiment in the white labor movement. Northern white labor saw the threat of competition for jobs from the fugitive slaves and the potentially millions behind them if abolition prevailed in the South. There was considerable racism toward freed Blacks in the North.

The most downtrodden sector of white workers—the immigrants—might seem to have had the least stake in white supremacy. But the racism had its strongest expression among these sections because at the bottom layer of white labor, they felt most intensely the competition from Blacks for jobs,[7] and blamed Blacks for their low wages. During the Civil War, the Irish and other immigrant workers were the base for the "anti-draft" riots in the Northern cities. These were really straight out murderous race riots against the local Black population.

For DuBois, the position of the Northern working class appears somewhat irrational. Freed slaves did represent, it's true, potential competition for jobs. However, DuBois argues, "What they [white workers] failed to comprehend was that the black man enslaved was an even more formidable and fatal competition than the black man free." (p. 20)

This analysis seems inadequate. As materialists we have to wonder why such a formidable consensus[8] of a class and its organizations would hold a position over a long period of time that was opposed to their interests. In addition to the issue of competition, we must ask if the super-exploitation of Black labor was used to provide some additional benefits for white labor—in a way, did the formation of the U.S. empire anticipate some of the basic oppressor/oppressed worker relations described by Lenin with the development of imperialism? Certainly the issue in relationship to the Native Americans is clear: genocide provided the land which allowed many white workers to "rise" out of their class (which also strengthened the bargaining power of remaining laborers). This reality firmly implanted one of the main pillars of white supremacy. There were undoubtedly also some direct benefits from the super-exploitation of slave labor for the white work-ing class that DuBois does not analyze. Data presented in *Settlers* indicates that white American workers earned much higher wages than their British counterparts.

DuBois sees the material basis of white labor antag-onism to Blacks as based in competition for jobs and its impact on wage levels. On the other hand he sees the exis-tence of a slave strata as even worse competition. But how did this second aspect play itself out? Perhaps as direct competition only for the white working class in the South. But here there was the counterforce of slavery being the direct basis for a large section of whites to become petty bourgeois, while others got jobs overseeing and controlling Black labor. It isn't clear how slavery in the South would directly compete with Northern labor—and on the con-trary some benefits might be passed on as a result of the super-exploitation of Black labor. Certainly, first the wealth generated by King Cotton, and then the availability of the cheap raw materials, were cornerstones of the Northern industrialization that provided and expanded jobs.

Further, this issue cannot be treated in isolation from the other main pillar of white supremacy—the availability of land based on genocide of the Native Americans. It is doubtful that the capitalist class would have opened up the West for settlement without a guarantee of still hav-ing an adequate supply of cheap labor for industrialization. Earlier in England, to prepare the way for manufacture, there had been the brutal enclosure movements which forced peasants off the land in order to create a large sup-ply of cheap labor. In North America, the movement was in the opposite direction: people were actually settling the land, becoming peasants, while manufacture was developing. It is unlikely this would have been allowed without (1) slavery to guarantee cheap labor for the main cash crops and raw materials, and (2) an influx of immigrant labor into the Northern cities.

In any case, the predominant position among Northern labor opposed the spread of slavery but did not favor abolition; these positions were punctuated by occasional race riots with a white working-class base. In addition to the aspiration to rise to the petty bourgeoisie, a labor aristocracy began to develop in the prewar period, usually based in longer established white settlers as opposed to the immigrant workers. After 1850, unions of skilled labor began to separate from common labor. These skilled unions established closed shops that excluded Blacks and farmers.

After the Civil War, the defeat of the slavocracy, the presence of the Union Army, the reality of thousands of armed Black troops, all should have created radically new conditions and possibilities for Black/poor white alliance in the South. DuBois, in his very positive view of Reconstruction, goes so far as to describe it as "a dictatorship of labor" (p. 187) in the South. Reconstruction with the important Black role in Southern politics, did mean a lot of democratic reforms while it lasted. There are some significant indications of poor whites allying. For example, early on in Reconstruction, Mississippi and South Carolina had popular conventions with significant poor white involvement. The Jim Crow laws, later passed in Mississippi, found it necessary to place severe strictures against whites associating with Blacks. But there isn't much evidence of a solid alliance from any large sector of poor whites.

The basis for an alliance seems clear. The basic problem of Reconstruction was economic; the kernel of the economy was land. Both freed slaves and poor whites had an interest in acquiring land. It would seem logical to have an alliance to expropriate the old plantation owners.

DuBois gives several reasons why this alliance didn't come to fruition: (1) Poor whites were determined to keep Blacks from access to the better land from which slavery had driven the white peasants (i.e., if people took over ownership of land they had worked, the ex-slaves would get the choice plantation land.) (2) Poor whites were afraid that the planters would control the Black vote and thus be able to politically defeat the poor whites' class aspirations. (3) Petty bourgeois whites still wanted to have cheap Black labor to exploit. (4) White labor was determined to keep Blacks from work that competed with them; poor whites were desperately afraid of losing their jobs. (5) White labor, while given low wages, were compensated with social status, such as access to public parks, schools, etc.; the police were drawn from their ranks; the courts treated them leniently. In short, white labor saw a threat to their racial prerogatives in every advance of the Blacks.

These reasons were all very real. However, it is not clear on the face of it, why they should override the potential for joint expropriation of the plantation owners. We also must look at a factor that DuBois mentions but does not develop sufficiently, the power backing up Reconstruction was the Union Army. Despite the importance of Black troops, there is no indication that the Union Army as a structured institution was ever anything other than an instrument of Northern capital. Northern capital wanted to break the national political power of the old plantation owners (hence the Black vote) but they certainly didn't want to support the liquidation of private property, even in the South. In fact, by 1868 the Union Army had forcibly retaken almost all the plantation land seized and worked by communities of freed slaves. (See Vincent Harding, *There Is A River*.) Thus died the promise of "40 acres and a mule."

Thus, DuBois's characterization of Reconstruction as a "dictatorship of labor" backed by the Union Army seems overdrawn. He is much more on the mark when he says, "It was inconceivable, therefore, that the masters of Northern industry through their growing control of American government, were going to allow the laborers of the South any more real control of wealth and industry than was necessary to curb the political power of the planters ..." (p. 345)

It seems to me that with the presence and dominance of Union troops, the joint expropriation of the old plantations did not appear as a very tangible possibility. It is in that context, that the poor whites' overwhelming choice was to try to reconsolidate their old white privileges. (This would also be the natural spontaneous choice given the history and culture.) The power context also reflects on the question of alignments on a national scale.

Looking nationwide, DuBois reasons, "there *should* have been [emphasis added] ... a union between champions of universal suffrage and the rights of freedmen, together with the leaders of labor, the small landholders of the West, and logically the poor whites of the South" against the Northern industrial oligarchy and the former Southern oligarchy. (p. 239) This union never took place.

DuBois cites two main reasons: (1) The old anti-Black labor rivalry. (2) The old dream of becoming small farmers in the West becoming a dream of labor-exploiting farmers and land speculation.

Here again DuBois's explanation, while helpful, does not seem to be sufficiently materialist; the implication seems to be white workers going against their more basic material interest. We need to also specify some of the concrete benefits that accrued to white labor at the expense of Black (and Indian) subjugation. Also to reiterate, these choices took place in the context of a vigorous and rising U.S. capitalism. The prospect of white supremacist rewards that capitalists could offer must have seemed very real and immediate while the prospect of overthrowing private property (which would necessitate alliance with Blacks) must have seemed difficult and distant.

By the 1870s, the labor movement in the North saw the growth of craft and race unions. "Skilled labor proceeded to share in the exploitation of the reservoir of low-paid common labor" (p. 597). The position of common labor was greatly weakened since their strikes and violence could not succeed with skilled labor and engineers to keep the machinery going.

In the South, the poor whites became the shock troops for the mass terror that destroyed the gains of Black Reconstruction. DuBois explains that the overthrow of Reconstruction was a property—not a race—war. Still, the poor whites involved were not simply tools of property. They perceived their own interests in attacking the Black advances. In fact, some of the early examples of Klan-style violence that DuBois provides show such bands attacking the old planters as well as the freed slaves.

DuBois documents, state by state, the war of terror that defeated Reconstruction. Here, I will indicate it with one example: In Texas, during the height of the war, there were an average of sixty homicides per month. Black Reconstruction was also defeated with the complicity of Northern capital which was sealed with the withdrawal of Union troops in 1877. The defeat of Reconstruction meant that the color line had been used to establish a new dictatorship of property in the South. For Black labor, this meant a move back toward slavery in the form of sharecropping, Jim Crow laws, and violent repression. For white labor, their active support of the "color caste" (white supremacy) immeasurably strengthened the power of capital, which ruled over them.

3. Settlers: The Mythology
of the White Proletariat (J. Sakai)

While Allen and DuBois focus on specific periods, Sakai
sketches the whole period from the first European settlement to the current time. Also, Sakai examines the relationship of the white proletariat to Native Americans,
Mexicanos, and Asians, as well as to the Black nation.

This, of course, is quite a scope to cover in one book.
Sakai starts from an explicit political perspective: what
is called the "United States"…"is really a Euroamerican
settler empire, built on colonially oppressed nations and
peoples…" In this light, a lot is revealed about U.S. history
that is not only quite different from what we learned in
school but that also debunks interpretations generally put
out by the white Left.

Even for those of us who think we understand the
white supremacist core of U.S. history, reading *Settlers* is
still quite an education. To take one stark example, when
the Europeans first arrived there were an estimated 10 million Natives in North America. By 1900, there were only
300,000. Sakai also critiques the white supremacist nature
of movements mythologized by the Left such as Bacon's
Rebellion, Jacksonian Democracy, and the struggle for the
eight-hour work day. Sakai shows that integral to most

advances of "democratic" reform for white workers was an active consolidation of privileges at the expense of colonized Third World peoples.

In covering such a range, there are some points of interpretation that could be questioned. Overall it is a very revealing and useful look at U.S. history. For this review, I just want to look at one period, the 1930s. Then we also will examine the overall political conclusions that Sakai draws.

The Depression of the 1930s was a time of intensified class struggle, the building of the CIO,[9] the famed sit-down strikes such as Flint, the height of the Communist Party USA. The CIO of this period has often been praised by leftists as exemplary in including Black workers in its organizing drive.

Sakai sees the essence of the period as the integration of the various European immigrant minorities into the privileges of the settler nation (white Amerika). In return, as U.S. imperialism launched its drive for world hegemony, it could depend upon the armies of solidly united settlers (including the whole white working class) serving imperialism at home and on the battlefield. The New Deal ended industrial serfdom and gave the European "ethnic" national minorities integration as Amerikans by sharply raising their privileges—but only in the settler way: in government-regulated unions loyal to U.S. imperialism.

Where the CIO organized Black workers it was utilitarian rather than principled. By the 1930s Black labor had come to play a strategic role in five industries (usually performing the dirtiest and most hazardous jobs at lower pay): automotive, steel, meat packing, coal, railroads. Thus, in a number of industrial centers, the CIO unions could not be secure without controlling Afrikan (Black) labor. "The CIO's policy, then, became to promote integration under settler leadership where Afrikan labor was numerous and strong (such as the foundries, the meat packing plants, etc.) and to maintain segregation and Jim Crow in situations where Afrikan labor was numerically lesser and weak. Integration and segregation were but two aspects of the same settler hegemony." (p. 201)

At the same time, it was CIO practice to reserve the skilled crafts and more desirable production jobs for white (male) workers. For example, the first UAW/GM contract that resulted from the great Flint sit-down strike contained a "noninterchangibility" clause which in essence made it illegal for Black workers to move up from being janitors or foundry workers. Such policy came on the heels of Depression trends that had forced Blacks out of the better jobs. Between 1930 and 1936 some 50% of all Afrikan skilled workers were pushed out of their jobs.

Roosevelt's support of the CIO came from a strategy to control and channel the class struggle. A significant factor in the success of the 1930s union organizing drives was the government's refusal to use armed repression. No U.S. armed forces were used against Euro-Amerikan workers from 1933 to 1941.[10]

This policy was in marked contrast to, for example, the attack on the Nationalist party in Puerto Rico. In 1937, one month after President Roosevelt refused to use force against the Flint sit-down strike, U.S. police opened fire on a peaceful nationalist parade in Ponce, Puerto Rico. Nineteen Puerto Rican citizens were killed and over 100 wounded. While leftists committed to the organizing of the '30s might want to bring in different examples and argue Sakai's interpretations, I think that overall the subsequent history of the CIO has been clear: it has both reinforced white monopolies on preferred jobs and has been a loyal component of U.S. imperial policy abroad.[11]

What conclusions about the white working class can we draw from this history? Sakai takes a definite and challenging position. *Settlers* is addressed, internally, for discussion among Third World revolutionaries. Still, it is important for us to grapple with its politics and to apply those lessons to our own situation and responsibilities.

Sakai's general view of the history is that the masses of whites have advanced themselves primarily by oppressing Third World people—not by any means of class struggle. Also that for most[12] of U.S. history the proletariat has been a colonial proletariat, made up only of oppressed Afrikan, Indian, Latino, and Asian workers. On top of this basic history, U.S. imperial hegemony after World War II raised privileges to another level. "Those expansionist years of 1945–1965 ... saw the final promotion of the white proletariat. This was an en masse promotion so profound that it eliminated not only consciousness, but the class itself." (p. 319)

Thus, for Sakai, there is an oppressor nation but it doesn't have a working class, at least not in any politically meaningful sense of the term. To buttress this position Sakai, (1) discusses the supra-class cultural and ideological unification in the white community; (2) points to the much higher standard of living for white-Americans; and (3) presents census statistics to indicate that whites are predominantly (over 60%) bourgeois, middle-class, and labor aristocracy. Here, Sakai enumerates class based solely on white male jobs in order to correct for situations where the woman's lower status job is a second income for the family involved. This method, however, fails to take account of the growing number of families where the woman's wages are the primary income. The methodological question also relates to the potential for women's oppression to be a source for a progressive current within the white working class.

In a way, Sakai puts forward a direct negation of the opportunist "Marxist" position that makes class designation everything and liquidates the distinction between oppressed and oppressor nation.

Sakai's survey of U.S. history understates the examples of fierce class struggle within the oppressor nation which imply at least some basis for dissatisfaction and disloyalty by working whites. Still, these examples—defined primarily around economic demands and usually resolved by consolidation of privileges relative to Third World workers—cannot be parlayed into a history of "revolutionary class struggle."

Class consciousness cannot be defined solely by economic demands. At its heart, it is a movement toward the revolutionary overthrow of capitalism. "Proletarian internationalism"—solidarity with all other peoples oppressed and exploited by imperialism—is a necessary and essential feature of revolutionary class consciousness. In our condition, this requires up front support for and alliance with the oppressed nations, particularly those within the U.S. (Black, Mexicano, Native). Thus white supremacy

37

and class consciousness cannot peacefully co-exist with each other. One chokes off the other. An honest view of the 350-year history clearly shows that the alignment with white supremacy has predominated over revolutionary class consciousness.

Furthermore, the culture of a more or less unified, supra-class, white supremacist outlook is also a very important factor. That culture is a reflection of a common history as part of an oppressor nation; it also becomes a material force in perpetuating that outlook and those choices. Common culture is a format to organize even those whites with the least material stake in white supremacy.

All the above considerations, however, do not provide a complete class analysis. There are other aspects of people's relationship to the mode of production which are important. A central distinction is between those who own or control the means of production (e.g., corporations, banks, real estate) and families who live by wages or salaries, i.e., by working for someone else. Those who live by the sale of labor power have little control or access to the basic power that determines the purpose of production and the direction of society as a whole. In the best of times, most white workers may feel comfortable; in periods of crisis, the stress might be felt and resolved on qualitatively different lines within the oppressor nation (e.g., which class bears the costs of an imperialist war or feels the brunt of economic decline). Even among whites, those who aren't in control have a basic interest in a transformation of society. It may not be expressed in "standard of living" (goods that can be purchased) as much as in the quality of life (e.g., war, environment, health, and the impact of racism, sexism, decadence). Crises can bring these contradictions more to the surface, expressing the necessity to reorganize society.

In my view there definitely is a white working class. It is closely tied to imperialism; the labor aristocracy is the dominant sector, the class as a whole has been corrupted by white supremacy; but, the class within the oppressor nation that lives by the sale of their labor power has not disappeared. This is not just an academic distinction; under certain historical conditions it can have important meaning.

A dialectical analysis goes beyond description to look at both the process of development and the potential for transformation. This is the great value of the Ted Allen essays. They show how white supremacy was a conscious construction by the ruling class under specific historical conditions. This implies that, under different historical conditions, there also can be a conscious deconstruction by oppressed nations, women, and the working class. Our analysis has to look for potential historical changes and movement activity that could promote revolutionary consciousness within the white working class.

In approaching such an analysis, we must guard against the mechanical notion that economic decline will in itself lessen racism. The lessons from DuBois's description of the "anti-draft" riots of the 1860s (as well as our experience over the last twenty years) shows the opposite to be true. Under economic pressure, the spontaneous tendency is to fight harder for white supremacy. While the absolute value of privilege might decrease, the relative value is usually increasing as Third World people abroad and within the U.S. bear the worst hardships of the crisis. The white workers closest to the level of Third World workers can be the most virulent and violent in fighting for white supremacy.

Rarely have major sectors of the white working class been won over to revolutionary consciousness based on a reform interest. Imperialism in ascendancy has been able to offer them more bread and butter than the abstraction of international solidarity. But a more fundamental interest could emerge in a situation where imperialism in crisis can't deliver and where the possibility of replacing imperialism with a more humane system becomes tangible.

Some Lessons From The Sixties (1991)

In the '60s and '70s, it appeared as though the rapid advance of national liberation was remaking the world in the direction of socialism. In the past twelve years, the painful setbacks, have shown just how difficult it is to create a viable alternative to underdevelopment in the Third World. Today we are in an historical juncture of crisis in social practice and theory. Nonetheless, given prevailing conditions, the contradictions and social struggles are likely to continue to be most intense in the Third World. Now, however, we have no clear guidelines as to when, how, or even if these struggles can lead to socialism in the world.

While it is discouraging to no longer have a defined outline for the triumph of world revolution, the human stake in the outcome of the social crises and struggles does not allow us the luxury of demoralization. We have to make our most intelligent and concerted effort to maximize the potential for humanitarian and liberatory change.

Solidarity with the Third World struggles has to become our top priority for both humanitarian and strategic reasons—the more we can do to get imperialism off their backs, the better the chances for their potential for leadership toward world transformation to bloom. But solidarity cannot be ethereal, it cannot be developed and sustained with any scope without some sort of social base within the oppressor nation. Class may very well not be a primary form for such a social base, but we still need to establish more realistic and useful terms for the role class can play in the next period of social upheaval and motion. The historical lessons we examined make it clear that it would be unreal to talk about the white working class "as a whole," or even the majority of it, as a revolutionary force. But, on the other hand, the predominance of white supremacy is not genetically determined nor is it carved in stone historically. We need to look for what conditions and movement activity can promote anti-imperialist organizing within the white working class—both to build solidarity forces and to point the direction toward a genuine long-term emancipation of working people from a system based on exploitation, dehumanization, and war.

The movement of the 1960s showed the potential for positive response from whites to the rise of national liberation struggles, along with a desire for a more humane and cooperative society. It is true that this response came first from elite students, the children of the petty bourgeoisie and professionals. These sectors felt more secure in their privilege and felt less immediately threatened by advances for Black people than did the poorer sectors of whites. Also, students and intellectuals are frequently the group that early on, albeit subjectively, responds to emerging contradictions in a given society. The movement was a real reflection of the objective advance of national liberation and the need to transform U.S. society. As the war in Vietnam dragged on, increasing numbers of working-class youth became involved in the movement.

This fledgling success and glimmer of potential of the '60s also provided some historical lessons that we have not done nearly enough to analyze and codify. The movement involved more than the traditional unrest of students. Broader cultural identification played a major role in generating a larger youth movement. First and foremost it was the impact of Black culture, with its more humane values of social consciousness, emotional expressiveness, and sense of community—primarily through the genesis of rock 'n roll. The cultural rebellion also importantly involved an opening of sexual expression that challenged the prevailing straitjacket of repression. Paradoxically, to the grim realities we've come to understand, at that time drugs (particularly marijuana and LSD) were seen as liberation from repressive control and promoting anti-authoritarianism.

Civil rights and anti-war activity among whites started mainly on the campuses, and the student movement was a spearhead for political consciousness throughout the '60s. Most white working-class youth were initially indifferent if not downright hostile to these initial stirrings. But over the years there were increasing cultural links that laid the basis for a broader movement. For example, white working-class youths who dropped out of the daily work grind and were often into drugs, gravitated to communities near campuses. Anti-draft counselling offices brought many into more direct, political contact with the movement. The burgeoning of community colleges meant that more working-class youth were themselves students. By the late 1960s the growing disenchantment and anger about the war in Vietnam provided a unifying focus and sense of identity for all the disaffected. When soldiers in Vietnam started to turn against the war, that added a new dimension to the movement, as well as significantly deepening its class composition.

The main base for the anti-imperialist movement of the '60s was a social movement of youth, heavily impacted and in many ways generated by Black culture. As the movement developed, it involved increasing numbers of working-class youth, who played a major role in the movement's growth and heightened militancy. This extension showed, (1) the ability of culture to be a bridge to deepening the class base of a social movement; (2) the increasing ways the draft, in the context of a bloody and losing war, made the interests of some working-class people intersect with those of national liberation; (3) the contagious effect of victorious revolutions and liberatory vision.

The New Left did have an intelligent strategy for extending the movement and deepening its class base, but abandoned it at the very moment it was achieving stunning success. The Revolutionary Youth Movement (RYM) strategy called for the extension of what had started as a primarily elite student base to a broader, particularly working-class, youth base by doing more work around the draft, with G.I.s, in community colleges, and among youth in working-class neighborhoods. The movement, still heavily male supremist, had little sense of the role of women and often lapsed into very negative sexist posturing. However even here the freedom energy and rhetoric of the movement provided a new opening for women's liberation. Women active in the Civil Rights Movement and in SDS (Students for a Democratic Society) provided a major impetus for the new wave of feminism that emerged in 1967. Unfortunately, the reaction of men within the movement was so sexist that it led to what has become an ongoing and destructive stasis that pits anti-imperialism and women's liberation against each other. But RYM did offer a vision extending the movement to involve broader working-class sectors without losing the political focus on anti-war, anti-racism, and militancy.

Large numbers of working-class youth did get involved in the movement. At the high point, millions took to the streets in the wake of the 1971 invasion of Cambodia and the killing of students at Kent State. This movement was of course not magically free of racism, as painfully illustrated by the failure to make issues of the killings at Jackson State and of Chicano anti-war activists in Los Angeles. But it was a movement that could, with political leadership, have strong anti-imperialist potential.

SDS, which correctly formulated the RYM strategy in December, 1968, was already splintered apart by May 1971. The dissolution of SDS shortly before the triumph of its strategy was not simply a question of stupidity or even just a matter of the pervasive power of opportunism. The student movement had reached a crisis in 1969 because its very successes had moved it from simply "shocking the moral consciousness of America" to realizing it was in fundamental opposition to the most powerful and ruthless ruling class ever. The murderous attacks on the Black movements we supported (dozens of Black activists were killed and a couple of thousand incarcerated from 1968 through 1971) drove the point home graphically at the same time that the dictates of solidarity urgently pressed us to qualitatively raise our level of struggle. The movement went into a crisis in 1968 because it came face to face with the terrifying reality of imperialism's power.

RYM was a creative and realistic strategy to extend the base and power of the movement, although it needed to be joined by an equally strong politics on women's liberation. But for all of its value as a transitional strategy, RYM was of course in itself nowhere near an adequate basis for overthrowing bourgeois power. So, looking for immediate answers in the crisis, the Left floundered on the perennial dilemma in white supremist society. The majority looked for a magic solution to the problem of power by mythicizing the white working class (the majority in the U.S.) as "revolutionary"—in reality this position meant a retreat into white supremacy and away from confronting imperialism. The minority tried to maintain purity around racism and the war by seeing ourselves as exceptional whites, separated from any social base—in reality this position meant abandoning responsibility for building a movement that could sustain militant struggle against imperialism.

While a youth movement in itself can't be sufficient, the promising success of RYM within its realm does suggest some lessons:

(1) the role culture can play in building cross-class movements;

(2) the value of looking for potential points of intersection of interests of whites with the advance of national liberation—e.g., (a) costs of imperialist wars, G.I.'s, draft, taxes, social priorities; (b) situations of common oppression where there is Third World leadership (welfare, prisons, some labor struggles); and (c) situations where a

vision of a revolutionary alternative can be most readily perceived (youth, women);

(3) the likelihood that social movements can play more of a role in involving white working people in a progressive struggle than traditional, direct forms of class organizing. The social movements though—youth, Lesbian-Gay-AIDS, anti-war and anti-nuclear, ecology, and potentially around housing, health, and education—have typically had a "middle-class" leadership and a primarily middle-class base. ("Middle-class" meaning people from college educated backgrounds—mainly professionals and petty bourgeois.)

While the Women's movement is usually labeled as a social movement because it is not one of the traditional struggles for state power, it should be more appropriately grouped with national liberation and class as responding to one of the three most fundamental structures of oppression. No movement can be revolutionary and successful without paying full attention to national liberation, class content, and the liberation of women. After the collapse of the anti-war and youth movements in the '70s the women's movement provided the most sustained and extensive impetus for social change within white America. Like the social movements, the leadership and main active base was middle-class. With the ebbing of the radical women's liberation tendency that identified with national liberation, the apparent leadership of contemporary feminism has a more pronounced middle-class character—at the same time that many more working-class women, while eschewing the name "feminism," have actively adopted and adapted the goals and struggles of the movement.

We would argue that the women's movement and the social movements, to be revolutionary, must relate to racism, national liberation, and Third World leadership. But we should add that, as with the youth movement, each should be looking for ways to extend its base into the working class on an anti-racist and pro-women's liberation basis.

The Lesbian-Gay-AIDS movement has been of particular urgency, militancy, and importance in this period. The struggle around AIDS has pushed the radical sector toward the need to ally with Third World and poor white communities impacted by intravenous drugs and poor healthcare. The AIDS movement has also provided leadership in breaking through the sterile conservative (cut back services to the poor) versus liberal (defend state bureaucracy) definition of political debate. ACT UP and others have provided an excellent example of mobilization and empowerment from below for self-help while at the same time demanding a redistribution of social resources to meet these social needs.

Peace, ecology, the homeless, healthcare, education all speak to important pieces that express the inhumanity and ineffectiveness of the whole system. Of course these movements have been, almost by definition, reformist. But that doesn't mean that they have to be under all circumstances: e.g., (1) a deeper crisis in imperialism where it has less cushion from which to offer reforms; (2) a situation where revolutionary alternatives are strong enough to be tangible; (3) a political leadership that pushes these movements to ally with national liberation, promote women's liberation, and deepen their class base, while at the same time drawing out the connections among the different social movements into a more coherent and overall critique of the whole system. Under such circumstances and leadership, the social movements could not only involve far more white working-class people in anti-systemic struggles, but would also serve to redefine and revitalize class issues and class struggle itself.

Lessons from the '60s certainly don't offer a blueprint for the '90s, which are a very different decade. Clearly we are not now in a period of progressive social upheaval. Economic dislocation, at least initially, provides fertile ground for white supremacist organizing. National liberation struggles are not at this point achieving a clear path to socialism.

What is certain is that there will be changes, and, at points, crises. We can't afford to repeat the old errors of once again floundering on the dilemma of either "joining" the working class's white supremacy or of abandoning our responsibility to organize a broader movement. While there is no blueprint, the basis for a real starting point is an analysis of actual historical experience.

In sum, revolutionaries must be realistic about the history of white supremacy, the impact of material wealth and dominance, and the mushrooming of job and status differentials among workers, both nationally and internationally. There is nothing approximating the Marxist revolutionary proletariat within white America. At the same time, the distinction between those who control the means of production and those who live by the sale of labor power has not been completely obliterated.

A system of white supremacy that was historically constructed can be historically deconstructed. A key factor for whites is the tangibility of a revolutionary alternative as opposed to the more immediate relative privileges that imperialism has had to offer. In this regard we have no map of what the future will bring. The experience of the '60s does offer some possible lessons for when the system is under stress. (1) Anti-imperialist politics are more important than initial class composition. (2) Culture, especially with ties to Third World people, can be an important force for building progressive cross-class movements. (3) In seeking to extend such movements, revolutionaries should look for intersection points of white working-class interests with the advance of national liberation, such as the draft. (4) Women's liberation must play a central role in all movements we build. (5) The various social movements, if we can fight for an alliance with the national liberation movements and the presence of women's politics and leadership, can be important arenas for extending our base to include working-class people, mutually redefine class and social issues, and make the connections to an overall anti-systemic perspective.

After the Sixties:
Reaction and Restructuring (2017)

The three decades following World War II are often referred to as the "golden age" of capitalism. Those who proclaim it so disregard the millions of people worldwide who suffered from hunger, deprivation, and abuse. The reference is to that period's high rates of economic growth and steep gains in real wages in the U.S., especially for white, male workers. This economic strength was based in no small part on U.S. dominance in the world economy. Unsurprisingly, most of the white working class, especially the dominant unions, maintained loyalty to the U.S.'s imperial mission.

By the early 1970s, in a reversal of the alchemists' dreams, the gold started to turn into lead, with imperialism besieged around the world and at home and with the emergence of some intractable economic problems. The turmoil led to some major restructuring economically and politically, with heavy impact on the white working class in the U.S. The impressive gains in real wages were forcibly reined in and levelled off, while jobs and benefits were made less secure. Those changes were accompanied by the ramping up of the politics of racial scapegoating. These developments took place in the context of the broader crisis for imperialism and the fierce counterattacks it launched.

Imperialism was in many ways on the ropes internationally. At center stage, the mightiest military machine in world history was being defeated by Vietnam, a poor Third World (Global South) country. At the same time, dozens of national liberation struggles were raging throughout Africa, Asia, and Latin America, threatening to end the huge profits and strategic raw materials the transnational corporations raked in from the labor and resources there at obscenely cheap rates. The sweep of revolutions, the potential for "two, three, many Vietnams" as Che Guevara put it, threatened to overextend and defeat imperialism. Much of the U.S. public, including many soldiers, came to actively oppose such military interventions.

Inspired by the decolonization of Africa, Black people, Native Americans, Puerto Ricans, Chican@s, and Asian-Americans launched militant struggles for self-determination. They all, especially the Black Liberation Movement, inspired a range of emerging radical upsurges: antiwar, G.I. (soldier) resistance, students, women, lesbian/gay (now expanded and referred to as LGBTQ), environmental, younger workers' labor militancy. Many of these movements involved some, and increasing numbers of, younger white working-class people.

Revolutions throughout the Third World threatened to cut off imperialism's most lucrative—and absolutely necessary—arenas of exploitation. Insurgencies at home also began to seriously erode profits: the federal government sought to co-opt the Black struggle with welfare programs that required tax dollars; environmental protection entailed new demands and costs for industry; women, whose wages were only 59% of those for men, were demanding equality; younger workers set off a wave of wildcat strikes (i.e., unauthorized by the union) with the potential for sparking widespread militancy that would raise labor costs.

As it happened, these political challenges mounted at the same time as another economic blow: competition from Europe and Japan. Those economies had been in rubble at the end of World War II but were now rebuilt, with technologically advanced production turning out competitive goods for the world market. U.S. industries faced increasing difficulties in selling their full output at the prices they expected. In 1971, the U.S. experienced its first trade deficit since the late 1800s, the beginning of what would become a chronic and mounting imbalance.

This cascade of challenges had a severe impact on the bottom line. The average profit rate in the U.S. fell from almost 10% in 1965 to 4.5% in 1974.[13] While profit rates can vary considerably with cyclical ups and downs, these setbacks were deeper and more long term—what Left economists term a "structural crisis." The most dramatic early sign came in 1971, when President Nixon shocked the world by unilaterally cancelling the direct international convertibility of (the right to redeem) the United States dollar to gold. The fixed peg of $35 for an ounce of gold had been a foundation piece of world finance since the end of World War II. Soon the U.S. economy began to suffer troubling inflation (big price increases) and stagnation (serious slowdown in economic growth) at the same time. This "stagflation" posed a new and dire dilemma for capital because it defied and discredited the standard Keynesian techniques for economic management. Governments were supposed to run budget deficits, thereby pumping money in, to stimulate a stagnating economy. Conversely, they were supposed to run budget surpluses, thereby taking money out, to cool off inflation. What were they to do now that the economy raced off in both of these supposedly opposite directions at the same time?

The situation was made even worse by the "oil shocks" as OPEC (Organization of Petroleum Exporting Countries) drove up the cost of a barrel of oil from $3 to $31 in the course of the decade. Of course these hikes were also very profitable for the big oil companies, but they became major cost factors for other industries. OPEC conjured up a ghastly spectre for corporate America: what if the wave of national liberation led a range of Third World producers of essential raw materials to band together to raise prices?

Naturally, with such vast wealth and power at stake, the lords of the global economy were not going to take this series of blows lying down. Their think tanks and political representatives developed a set of momentous and viciously destructive strategies to restructure political rule and economic dominance in their favor. These efforts included a number of ways to reduce labor costs at home. Before getting to that, I want to briefly sketch three other main areas. Each of these efforts entailed concerted, companion propaganda and cultural campaigns, which I won't take the time to describe beyond an occasional example.

1. Wrecking National Liberation

Even though it was not an especially lucrative source of wealth, the U.S. doggedly pursued the war on Vietnam based on the "domino theory." One Third World country falling out of the imperial orbit might set off a series of others once they saw it could be done. That's why imperialism couldn't allow any national liberation movement to become an attractive example of how much better things could be for their people. For that reason, long after the U.S. realized it would have to leave Vietnam and the neighboring Indo-Chinese countries of Laos and Cambodia, it rained down the most extensive and concentrated bombings in world history. It also pursued an unprecedented program of ecocide using twenty million gallons of herbicides, mainly the highly toxic Agent Orange. These crimes against humanity not only presented overwhelming immediate obstacles to achieving a healthy and thriving Vietnam; they continue to take a cruel toll on the people and economy to this day, more than forty years later.

Imperialism also had to find ways to derail national liberation where they couldn't just send in the marines. They developed a two-pronged strategy. (a) The CIA fostered and sponsored armed terrorist groups such as the "Contras" in Nicaragua, UNITA in Angola, and RENAMO in Mozambique. These gangs inflicted random, brutal violence against civilians; they also targeted rural health and education workers in particular in order to destroy the gains made by the revolutions. (b) The U.S. and its allies often imposed economic embargoes, which cut these countries off from the machinery and components needed to build an integrated economy, as well as medicines and other products necessary for the population's well-being. The combination of these two forms of attack turned back many of the impressive initial gains in literacy, healthcare, women's rights, and mass political participation. Chaos and poverty reigned instead.

2. Kicking the "Vietnam Syndrome"

You can't keep an extortion racket going if the victims can opt out without repercussions. While the above tactics were often effective, the U.S. couldn't give up the option of direct military intervention. But the U.S. public was no longer willing to support such wars. That was called the "Vietnam Syndrome." The ruling class made getting past that distaste for war a top priority. To do so, they organized a series of stepping stones, each one on false pretenses, to give citizens renewed confidence that such aggressions could be carried out with minimal U.S. casualties and economic costs. In 1983, in an action similar to a pro boxer picking a fight with an infant, the U.S. invaded Grenada, a tiny country of 100,000 people. In 1989, moving up to a toddler, they sent troops into Panama, a country of a little over three million (one hundredth of the U.S.'s size). In 1991 they took on an adolescent with an all-out war on Iraq, a country of thirty million. Preceding that invasion, the media carried on with all kinds of hype about how powerful the Iraqi army was—all designed to make the inevitable U.S. victory seem all the more impressive. That invasion was devastating for the people of Iraq but had little cost for the U.S., where it was glorified in the Pentagon-guided media. After the big bully prevailed, President George H.W. Bush couldn't contain himself and publicly gloated, "We kicked the Vietnam Syndrome!" Then, in the course of the 1990s, NATO's air forces showed how much could be accomplished without "boots on the ground," as concerted bombings of Yugoslavia reduced that multinational state, which had resisted some of the dictates of the world market, to a fragmented set of hostile ethnic enclaves.

Today U.S. imperialism is happily wallowing in the filth of multiple never-ending brutal wars—Afghanistan, Iraq, Libya, Somalia, Yemen, Syria. In every one of these situations the crisis was instigated in large part by U.S. interventions. None of them has a reasonable resolution in sight. All of them serve as steroids for the overblown military machine. Each one has been totally devastating for the people of the country involved.

The predominance of this kind of intervention is also a symptom of the decline of imperialism, with its greatly diminished ability to install stable puppet regimes in the Global South. So, it now regularly must resort to the fallback strategy of plunging potentially recalcitrant countries into terribly destructive chaos. Of course, those lives don't matter—never did—to imperialism.

The stepping stones back to an unbridled U.S. military segued into the unending, continuous, and brutal "war on terror." U.S. intervention itself created the unsavory groups that are now given as a justification for more intervention.

The extensive and growing use of drones has allowed the U.S. to carry out bombings, unambiguous acts of war, on some seven countries at this time, with no U.S. casualties. For theaters of combat where U.S. troops are still engaged, the government and media have relentlessly pursued a cultural standard where any criticism of a war is tantamount to an attack on the soldiers, "our brave men and women who are fighting for our freedoms." This canard turns reality totally upside down. The rulers who use working-class youth as cannon fodder in these wars of aggression are the ones disrespecting them, by putting them in harm's way as well as subjecting them to the trauma of inflicting violence on other human beings.

3. The War Against the Black Rebellion

Within the U.S, the Black rebellion was the most dramatic threat to those in power. At the same time as the U.S. was losing in Vietnam, widespread uprisings in the inner cities had the ruling class facing its nightmare of a two-front war. Also, the Black struggle was the spearhead for a range of radical movements. The government strategy to crush Black liberation had two main thrusts:

(*a*) They implemented an extensive counter-insurgency program designed to destroy radical Black organizations. While the FBI and various police forces had surveilled and disrupted the Civil Rights Movement, they moved into a full-court press against Black power with the August 25th, 1967, FBI memo that outlined a national program "[...] to expose, disrupt, misdirect, or otherwise neutralize the activity of black nationalist hate-type [sic] organizations or groupings [...]" The FBI's now notorious COINTELPRO (Counterintelligence Program) was only one of many illegal and often violent attacks carried out by a range of government agencies. The tactics included planting false "snitch" accusations to create bitter divisions, as well as outright assassinations. In 1969 alone, twenty-seven Black Panthers were killed and 749 were arrested. Similarly, some sixty American Indian Movement members and sympathizers on the Pine Ridge reservation were killed in the three years following the Indigenous takeover/reclaiming of Wounded Knee. (For a lot more on both of these COINTELPRO campaigns, see Ward Churchill and Jim Vander Wall, *Agents of Repression*.) Many Puerto Rican, Chican@, and a number of other activists were killed or put away with long prison sentences.

(b) The government also worked to incapacitate the broader Black community. The lead tactic here has been mass incarceration, on top of a number of health (including drugs), social, and economic assaults. The dramatic change can be seen in a chart of rates of imprisonment. For the fifty years preceding, the line is flat with a constant rate, comparable to other countries, of 100 prisoners per 100,000 people. Then in 1973 the line starts a breathtaking ascent, rising to 500 per 100,000—five times the previous rate—by 2005.[14] Within that gigantic overall figure, Black males are six times more likely than their white counterparts to be put in prison. One of several pistons driving this incarceration machine was the war on drugs. Those who promoted it already knew, from the 1917–33 experience with Prohibition, that such an effort was guaranteed to result in a mushroom cloud of "crime" and violence. The damage done by mass incarceration isn't just to those put behind bars but also to the larger community, which suffers from the removal of needed loved ones, breadwinners, and mentors. (The two-headed monster of political repression and mass incarceration is discussed in my pamphlet, "Our Commitment Is to Our Communities"; for a more in-depth account, see Elizabeth Kai Hinton, *From the War on Poverty to the War on Crime*.) Kali Akuno, in his brilliant essay "Until We Win," points out that there's a third prong. Corporations and the government have cultivated and then utilized sections of the Black petit bourgeoisie and working class to create class divisions within the Black community.

4. Reining in Labor Costs

The serious erosion of profit rates also led to a concerted capitalist campaign to contain labor costs at home. In 1970–71, labor unions launched the largest and most successful series of strikes in post-WWII U.S. history, winning huge gains for workers. Capital then used the 1973–75 recession, the worst since the 1930s, to wage a counter-offensive. Businesses began to shift, where possible, to nonunion workers and went to the courts to set limits on the number of pickets at a site and the use of secondary boycotts to support strikes.

The labor/management playing field was tilted, precipitously, by the Volcker interest rate hike of 1979. Paul Volcker, the chairman of the Federal Reserve, sent interest rates through the roof, up to 20%. The ostensible reason was to fight inflation, but the recession that inevitably followed led to an unemployment rate that reached 10.8% in 1981, a post-WWII high. This put labor in a very weak bargaining position, which enabled capital to implement significant restructuring.

Before looking at these changes we need to acknowledge how this manipulation ravaged the Third World. In the early 1970s, when interest costs were low, many of these countries took out large loans—a lot of which were spent by U.S.-supported dictators on military hardware or for vanity projects. Now that those rates were sky high, these countries couldn't even keep up on interest payments. The debt mushroomed, and that became the cudgel to impose in essence a global system of debt peonage, as the International Monetary Fund and the World Bank used it to mandate "structural adjustment programs" (SAPs) on over seventy countries. The SAPs were draconian austerity regimes, very favorable for the transnational corporations operating in the Third World and ruinous for the people and for economic development there. (For a fuller discussion, see the essay in my book, *No Surrender*, "The Global Lords of Poverty," which explains why, "There is probably no dynamic in motion today that has more devastating impact on more lives." This essay is also available online at the Kersplebedeb website.)

The most visible turning point for labor in the U.S. came with the PATCO strike. The Professional Air Traffic Controllers Organization went out on strike on August 3rd, 1981. In one of his earliest decisive actions, President Reagan dismissed them on August 5th and brought in replacement workers. (A week later he signed a law providing the biggest ever tax cuts for the rich.) Reagan's success in replacing even such highly skilled workers provided a clear example for private business; many companies, including Phelps Dodge (mining) and Greyhound (bus), soon followed suit. Job actions went from being a means of advancement for labor to the occasions for serious setbacks. The number of major strikes began its nosedive, from 286 a year at the end of the 1960s to 34 a year in the 1990s.

The shifting of manufacture to the Third World took off. By some accounts (these estimates are hard to do and can vary considerably) over two million jobs were lost to downsizing and globalization from 1979 to 1983.[15] Those losses have been accompanied by a rise of low-paying service jobs, such as Walmart, and increased use of temporary and part-time labor with minimal benefits. These changes made jobs a lot less secure, which heightened workers' anxieties and further weakened their bargaining power. Union negotiations often turned into labor "givebacks" in wages and benefits to try to keep jobs. (For a fuller summary of the impact of the Volcker shock, replacement workers, and the loss of manufacturing jobs, see Harold Meyerson's 2013 article "The Forty-Year Slump" available online at http://prospect.org/article/40-year-slump).

Unions are important not only for their members but also to set a better framework for all of labor. Union membership in the U.S. peaked in 1954 at 34.8% of all wage and salary workers. In 1983 it was at a respectable 20.1%; today it's an anemic 11.1%. But within that there is a disparity. In the private sector it's only 6.9%; the remaining stronghold is in the public sector, most notably teachers' unions. (Teachers as the last bulwark of unionism helps explain the heartwarming phenomenon of hedge fund billionaires becoming "education reformers"—promoting the proliferation of charter schools with nonunion teachers.)

This series of changes has had considerable impact. From 1947 to 1974, real wages (that is, with the numbers corrected for inflation) rose 95%. In the more than forty years since then, despite comparable gains in productivity[16], real wages have risen only a paltry 10%. For white male workers they remained completely flat: $20.78/hour in 1973, $21.03 in 2015. These figures average out a wide range of workers. Those at the bottom lost ground with a something like a one third decline for white male workers with no more than a high school education. This loss of income, security, and status has had a dire impact. In sharp contrast to long-term trends among all others in the U.S., these less educated white males are now experiencing a marked decline in life expectancy. This shocking outcome is evidently the result of a rise in drug addiction and suicides and of the physiological damage from stress.

Median family income rose 111% from 1945 to 1973, but only 9% since then. That's a little better than white male wages because more family members have entered the work force; also there have been some gains, although still far from equal, for women's wages. Perhaps even more important than these wage and income concerns is the new precariousness. Now many workers feel they could easily lose their jobs or be downgraded, which could have dire consequences for healthcare coverage or repaying student loans. On top of that injury, people get the infuriating insult of soaring inequality. In 1965, the CEOs at the 350 largest public U.S. firms made twenty times the pay of their average worker; by 2013, it was close to three hundred times.

The post-1973 economic changes have been summarized and analyzed a lot more fully by many authors on the Left, often in ways that seem to set the stage for the traditional Left vision of the workers rising up against the bosses. So far, the Right has had more success in capitalizing on white workers' frustrations. A tunnel vision focused on stagnating real wages and increased precariousness misses or downplays other crucial dimensions of reality: white supremacy, male supremacy, imperialism. At least on average, white male workers have not been pushed down to the level of mere subsistence or below; what their wages buy today is comparable to 1973. What's changed is that they no longer have the dazzling rise in their standard of living of the twenty-five years that followed World War II. Losing what felt like an entitlement became a catalyst for important cultural changes. Many white males who had felt on top of the world as far as workers are concerned began to feel besieged. The politics were framed in a way that they felt any gain for people of color or women as an attack on their own position in society. That sentiment got expressed in a distaste for "political correctness" and an intensified hatred for political elites who were making some concessions in order to co-opt the Black and other struggles. Some of us in the movement, in the spirit of Martin Luther King Jr.'s poor people's campaign, sought to include low-income whites in demands for affirmative action. There's evidence that political operatives in the Nixon administration maneuvered to make such programs race or gender-based only—in order to generate a white, male backlash.

Racial animus, sexism, America-First arrogance are so deeply embedded, so much in the very foundation of U.S. history and culture, that they can readily form the basis of reaction for many white working-class families when they feel stressed. That's not just "false consciousness." At least in the short and intermediate run it has a definite material basis. Hard times in the U.S. usually don't drive workers of all races into a common situation. The Black/white male wage gap had narrowed during the Civil Rights era. Then in the early 1970s it began to widen again to the point that it's now similar to what it was in the 1950s ... the Jim Crow era that is Donald Trump's reference point for "Make America Great Again." In 1973 the median hourly wage for Black male workers was about 77% of their white male counterparts; today it is 70%. The smaller gap among women narrowed from 80% to 87%, but since male wages are higher, overall Blacks have lost ground.

Household wealth is an even more telling measure than income. Wealth includes all assets such as cars, homes, savings, investments, while any debts would be a negative, a deduction. Wealth can be accumulated and passed on over generations and is crucial to whether people have something to fall back on in case of sickness, or to send someone to college, or to get a loan to start a small business. Black and Latin@ families were especially hard hit by the tsunami of home foreclosures following the financial crisis of 2008. The white/Black difference in this crucial index of security and well-being is staggering. The ratio of white to Black household wealth is a whopping 13 to 1.[17] The situation is not much better for Latin@s at 10 to 1.

We also live in a global and class polarized economy. According to a recent Oxfam study, the eight richest individuals, eight mega-billionaires, control as much wealth as the 3.6 billion poorest human beings. When we look at income and wealth, it's not just a matter of side-by-side figures. The colossal riches and abject poverty are two sides of the same global coin, as those on the top continue to suck up fabulous riches at the expense of labor, resources, and deprivations of those at the bottom. One example of how that wealth is generated can be found in the fire-trap garment factories in Bangladesh, where women work 70-hour weeks for $18.

In the U.S., women have made some wage gains relative to men, up to 79%—still grossly unequal and quite a rake-off for employers. But those women are likely to face the "double shift" of having jobs and also doing the bulk of the demanding but unpaid household work. It can be a triple shift when we include the way it often falls on women to provide emotional support and caring. At the same time, there's been a large increase in households headed by a single female. These families have by far the highest rate of poverty, an inexcusable 28.2%.

Sometimes we on the Left can sound dangerously close to the "America First" Right-wing when we denounce the export of manufacturing jobs. Those losses have hurt. At the same time, imperial globalization has been far more damaging for the three quarters of humanity who live in the Global South. SAPs have entailed reducing already abysmal wages and radically cutting back on government subsidies for the poor. "Free trade" has meant that goods pour in from heavily subsidized U.S. agribusiness, under-cutting and then eliminating the small farmers who were the backbone of the local economy. This process is one of the factors that have driven hundreds of millions of people off the land, creating massive unemployment and thereby a pool of people so desperate that they'll work—often at manufacture that was outsourced from the U.S.—at star-vation wages. One of the most promising revolutionary movements of the period has been the Zapatista National Liberation Army. In 1994, the Indigenous Mayan popula-tion of Chiapas, Mexico rose up against NAFTA and how imports from the U.S. were wiping out local corn farmers.

The impact of globalization on U.S. workers is com-plex and involves more than just the decline of manufac-ture. One benefit is the cheaper consumer goods imported from low-waged countries. Even more importantly, the colossal corporate wealth reaped from the cheap labor and raw materials of the Global South is used to build and sustain the burgeoning nonproductive sectors of the U.S. economy. By "nonproductive" I mean they don't provide for the survival and education of workers and their families and they don't provide equipment or techniques or mate-rials for production. In the U.S., the sales effort, including advertising, accounts for over $1 trillion. Military, security, and prisons come close to another trillion. The speculative aspects of FIRE (finance, insurance, and real estate) are much bigger still. As Zak Cope puts it in *Divided World, Divided Class*, "[...] if around 80% of the world's productive labor is performed in the Third World by workers earning less than 10% of the wages of First World workers, that provides not only for the profits of the *haute bourgeoisie* [capitalists] in the OECD [rich nations] but also the economic foundation for the massive expansion of retail, administration and security services." Many of those workers consider themselves to be of higher status than those who do physical labor and who often get dirty or exposed to toxins on their production jobs. The differences in status and the nature of work can be the basis for a more conservative politics and in any case add to the plethora of stratifications dividing those who live and support their families by working for wages or salaries.

While their frustrations and anxieties have increased, the white working class is situated in a contradictory position, both material and in light of the long political and cultural history. In this post-1973 period, the white/Black gap has actually increased. The wage difference between First World and Global South workers has narrowed a bit, but still is the size of Mount Everest, at 7 or 8 to 1. The transnational corporations and finance capital's huge rake-off from the Third World supports and provides jobs in the gigantic parasitic sectors of the U.S. economy. The benefits from imperial wealth affect the situation and consciousness even of many people of color in the U.S., leading some of them to support empire.

What has capitalism meant for the white working class over the past forty-five years? To put it in one sentence: stagnating real wages along with less job security, accompanied by a ramping up of the politics of racial scapegoating.

President Nixon built support for his lethal attacks on the Black liberation struggle with his cries of "Law and Order." In 1981, at the same time that President Reagan set about to break unions and provide record-breaking tax cuts for the rich, he publicly fulminated about "welfare queens" living high off of the taxpayer's dollar. Millions of white workers—"Reagan Democrats"—loved the movie actor as president because he socked it to the "[racial others]," even while he gutted labor's bargaining power. President Clinton ran on a promise to "end welfare as we know it," and signed an omnibus crime bill that greatly expanded the number of people in prison. These trends segued into the "war on terror" as the cattleprod to shock the public into supporting the warfare/security state; all of which has happened as income and wealth inequality has soared to unimagined heights in the U.S., and even more so in the world.

These developments set the stage for Trump, even if he doesn't, at this point, represent a consolidated ruling class strategy. He did lose the popular vote and also 40% of the electorate didn't vote at all. Nonetheless it is sobering that 63 million people, including large swaths of the working and middle classes,[18] voted for such a blatant racist and misogynist. That represents a strong potential base for virulent white nationalism.

We white radicals have a particular responsibility and crying need to organize as many white people as possible to break from imperialism and to see that their long term interests, as human beings and for a livable future for their children, lie in allying with the rest of humanity. The environmental and economic catastrophes we face can only be resolved by replacing capitalism with some form of socialism, based in commitment to community and harmony with nature. Class is one of several important elements of social reality. We can't organize by showing disdain or simply preaching; we need to engage people and hear their concerns. At the same time, we need to fully challenge the dominant politics and culture by articulating and representing a clear counterpoint to white supremacy. The importance of class does not mean we can just recite old formulas that abstract from the realities of imperialism, white supremacy, male supremacy—that abstract from the actual political history. Yet we have to find a way to get across to white working-class people the most fundamental issues: the only way to achieve a humane and sustainable society is by allying with the Global South and people of color.

Capitalism is inherently unstable. Right now the colossal concentration of wealth at the top is generating severe imbalances and the scope of financial speculation is creating steep vulnerabilities. There are bound to be times when conditions get even worse for millions of U.S. workers. Economic stresses or even depressions in themselves do not provide fertile soil for revolutionary consciousness to blossom. In the imperial nations, the dangers of economic crisis are likely to outweigh the opportunities unless we have reached large numbers beforehand on the basis of unity with the oppressed majority of humanity. That's why an urgent priority is to look for the places where movements for justice can best organize white people for their long term interests on an anti-imperialist, anti-racist, anti-sexist basis.

Many of the lessons from the 1960s still apply. Creating a visible rallying point for anti-imperialist politics is more important than the class composition, the percent that is working-class, that our movements start with. Cultural bridges can be an important force. What some on the Left have disdained as "social movements"—such as feminism, LGBTQ, environment—are not only important in their own right but might provide the best arenas, if we work consciously, to reach and involve working-class people. The large numbers of whites responding positively to Black Lives Matter, such as SURJ (Showing Up for Racial Justice) and other groups, is another important area to work for more of a working-class base.

The other major lesson from the 1960s is to look for places where white working-class folk can more immediately see how their interests intersect with struggles in the Third World and by people of color. Today we don't have the same level of casualties and costs as during the Vietnam War, although being in the military still can involve a lot of pain and trauma. Veterans for Peace have been vitally important; an especially inspiring recent example was when two thousand of them rallied to North Dakota, in front-line solidarity with the Standing Rock Sioux-led encampment against the oil pipeline. We very much need a strong antiwar movement, as the U.S. has been waging multiple wars, with criminal interventions that have turned whole nations into failed states. That devastation becomes the breeding ground for terrorist groups that in turn are used as the rationale for escalating the warfare/security state that is itself the main source of these conflicts.

In looking for intersection points, it helps to remember that the white working class is not the same as the U.S. working class. While the *white working class* within the U.S., which itself contains quite a variety of strata and politics, is an important demographic, the *U.S.* working class also encompasses many workers of color, including immigrants, who are doing much of the most arduous and exploited labor. One of the best places to organize white working-class people could well be in those arenas predominated and/or led by workers of color. Organizing home healthcare workers, campaigns for farmworkers, Justice for Janitors, the fight for a $15/hour minimum wage are current examples of such possibilities. These efforts often involve broader community mobilizations.

I am not offering, am not capable of, a grand strategy for organizing. But on top of the above lessons from the '60s, I want to stress two often neglected themes of overriding importance: internationalism and the environment. As differentiated and divided as the oppressed and exploited of the world may be, the vast majority have a fundamental interest in stopping capitalism's exterminationist assault on people and the environment. Several vitally needed ecosystems are on the brink of collapsing, thousands of species have been lost or are endangered, and now global warming is an existential threat to earth as a habitat for humanity. Environmental damage is caused mainly by the profligate economies of the North; the harm is most dire in the Global South. Any movement worth its salt must account for that differential.

But internationalism is not just a moral obligation; even more, it is the only path to victory. The Global South is where consciousness and struggles tend to be the most advanced; that is what gives us a chance against this Goliath of a ruling class. A telling example is what happened after the crucial 2009 international conference on climate change in Copenhagen failed to come up with a treaty. In response, many movements and nations of the Global South, along with their allies, met in Cochabama, Bolivia, and came up with a comprehensive, on-point People's Agreement that included strong statements on the Rights of Indigenous Peoples and the Rights of Mother Earth. While the environmental justice movement within the U.S. responded, there was otherwise all too little mobilizing here to create momentum for this outstanding program. Let's do better with the Eco-Socialism Conference slated to take place in Venezuela in November, 2017.

Even though the corporate media doesn't cover them, thousands of promising initiatives are in motion in the Global South—from peasant-led battles against destructive dams in India, to women-led fights for sustainable agriculture in Africa, to mass-based democratic challenges to capitalism in Latin America, to Indigenous efforts around the world to protect the water and Mother Earth. Our "Certain Days" Political Prisoner calendar of 2015 (www.certaindays.org) highlighted several examples. Naomi Klein's *This Changes Everything* provides many more.

Beyond encouraging people to adopt an internationalist perspective, we need to learn how to link up, how to make these issues concrete, how to organize. While I don't have a blueprint, I think that our broad approach can make a difference. The Left shouldn't try to outdo imperialism in promising workers at home a "higher standard of living." Instead, we have to show how we can work toward a better quality of life, especially for our children. That requires unity with the rest of humanity and harmony with nature. For example, Cuba's impressive advances around developing an ecological agriculture not only deserve our support but even more are an important example for us to learn from and apply.

Perhaps Trump's outrageous budget proposal can help us highlight the tradeoff between military aggression and social needs. We need pro-active programs that take some of the vast resources now harmfully squandered on the military, the sales effort, and financial speculation to instead create jobs that provide for the long term health of the planet. The geographic core of reactionary Donald Trump's electoral support was rural. Some of those areas would be well-suited for building a green economy with wind and/or solar power. We also want to work toward reparations to the Global South and communities of color. One form that could take is the development and transfer of green technology—not as a matter of guilt but as the way to join their leading efforts and to help all of us.

Within the U.S., the Jackson-Kush plan, led by the Malcolm X Grassroots Movement, offers a cogent way to build an economy around environmental projects, based on cooperatives, in the heart of the Black Belt in Mississippi.

Such an advanced program provides a strong context for trying to organize some working-class and poor whites as allies. Any successful efforts to build alternatives to rapacious capitalism will undoubtedly come under attack and must be supported in all the ways we can.

The current strongest expression of internationalism in the U.S. is solidarity with Palestine; the connections made with and by Black Lives Matter are especially moving. Palestine is a front-line struggle against settler colonialism and its enforcement through a form of apartheid. BDS (boycott, divestment, and sanctions) is an important and promising campaign that deserves our concerted support.

We urgently need a strong anti-war movement. Veterans for Peace, Veterans Against the War, and a number of other antiwar groups have provided a valiant beachhead, but it has been hard to build a mass movement in a period when the designated "enemies" have been so unsavory and U.S. casualties so low. But with an erratic and unpopular Commander-in-Chief anxious to prove how tough he is and with future terrorist incidents almost inevitable, we have to get across how U.S. aggressions have created a vicious spiral. We have to show how U.S. interventions to destroy the secular Lefts, to promote violent Islamist extremists, and then to turn whole countries into failed states are the combustion engine speeding this car off the cliff.

This reality also relates to the refugee and immigration crises that have served as highly combustible fuel for the racist arson squads of the U.S. and Europe's "populist" Right wings. The Left slogan of "No Borders" expresses our vision, but it skips over the more immediate, searing human reality. These crises are caused by how imperialism has ravaged Global South countries. Wealth extraction, military interventions, CIA operations, climate chaos pour across borders like devastating floods. These massive "migrations," these wholesale aggressions, have wrecked economies, generated pervasive violence, and undermined food production in the Middle East, Central America, and most of Africa. Our first and foremost task is to get the U.S. to respect the sovereignty—economic, political, military, and climate—of Indigenous peoples and Global South nations.

The only way to defeat the highly destructive capitalist globalization is with a deeply loving people's internationalism.

We live in a very dangerous time, but fortunately we have had a resurgence of activism in the U.S. over the past ten years, beginning with the massive mobilization for immigrants' rights in 2006. Occupy Wall Street helped define the real problem as the rule by the 1%. The LGBTQ movement has made impressive advances. Black Lives Matter and the Movement for Black Lives are confronting core injustices, and a growing number of anti-racist whites have been joining SURJ and other groups. The Native American encampment at Standing Rock to try to stop an oil pipeline that endangers the water supply is a powerful example of how Indigenous sovereignty can lead the struggles for environmental protection. These and other sparkling streams of struggle can be fed by a new torrent of anti-Trump protests to become a mighty and life-nurturing river.

We may not be able to organize the white working class as a whole, and a sector will fight against us. But there are positive ways to move forward. We can work for the "social movements" to become staunchly anti-imperialist and on that basis deepen the class base. And we can look for the ways to involve an increasing number of white working people in alliances with the forces that fight for justice and give us our only hope for a more humane and sustainable world.

Here's the haiku I wrote right after the 2016 election:

> Fierce volcanoes spew
> greed, hate. But six billion strong,
> we can fight and win.

Endnotes

1. As an aside, this background helps explain the rank dishonesty of the current debate on gun rights vs. control because both sides, in different ways, white-out the racial history. While liberals do express concern for the terrible toll guns take in oppressed communities, they won't challenge the damage capitalism has done and how that generates internal violence. The efforts for gun control don't break from racism because they push in the direction of a state monopoly, when the police are in many ways the modern day descendants of the slave patrols.

Conservative jurists who generally justify their positions by claiming that they stick to the original language and intent of the Constitution, make gun ownership an individual right. But the Second Amendment starts by framing the issue in terms of the need for well-regulated militias, and then talks of the right of "the people," not of "persons" (for individuals) to bear arms. Who were the militias?—their leading functions were to suppress slave rebellions, to act as slave patrols, and to lead the armed encroachments into Indigenous territories. This "right" was—and is—all about arming whites against Black and Native peoples.

There's a definite continuity to the inherent racism at the basis of these positions. When the Black Panthers displayed legal weapons in the 1960s, as a counter-force to police brutality, conservatives cried out for gun control. More recently, the right to bear legal arms didn't save Philando Castile from being killed by a policeman in Minnesota. There is a broad correlation between racist attitudes and opposition to gun-control laws. (See, George Zarnick, "Trump and the NRA," in *The Nation*, July 17–24, 2017.) While they won't say it openly the zeal to bear arms today, as well as opposing efforts to give the police a monopoly, is, as it was in 1790, mainly about whites having the lethal means of violence to use against people of color.

2. These figures come from reading a bar graph, so the numbers could be off by a percentage point either way. (See, Philip Bump, "There Probably Is No New Donald Trump Coalition," *Washington Post*, November 10th, 2016). The numbers don't add up to 100% because some people voted for other candidates. Other indicators of class, such as not having a college education, showed similar results. The dominant factor in voting patterns was race.

3. I don't discuss fascism in this paper. The term is tossed around in such a variety of ways that to use it meaningfully would require an essay in itself. To me, it is essential to situate the current dangers in the decline of imperialism. An essay that does a very good job of that is Michael Novick, "Fascism and How to Fight It." (http://ara-la.tumblr.com/post/72462635292/fascism-and-how-to-fight-it-from-2009)

4. There were several reasons why Blacks were the planters' choice for perpetual slavery. *(1)* After the English revolution of 1640–1666 the demand for labor expanded in England and limited the supply of English labor available to the colonies. *(2)* The alliance against feudalism that the English bourgeoisie had

by necessity forged with the lower classes limited their ability to impose wholesale slavery. (3) In the colonies, it would be harder for escaped Black slaves to blend in with the dominant white settler population.

5. He notes that Black historian Lerone Bennett, Jr. also developed the same basic analysis.

6. Many Black nationalists cite this period as when an oppressed Black (or New Afrikan) Nation was born within North America. This set of laws and color restrictions clearly went beyond the class exploitation of laborers to the systematic oppression of Afrikans as a people.

7. The most frequently cited examples of "competition" are Black workers lowering wages or, in later years, being used as strike breakers. But in reality the role of the white immigrants wasn't that passive. Before 1850, Black workers predominated in many trades in both Northern and Southern cities. A huge influx of white foreigners, particularly after the Irish famine in 1846, caused a radical change. The unskilled Irish, in particular, pushed Blacks out of these occupations. (C.F., Philip Foner, *Organized Labor & The Black Worker*, New York: 1982; p. 6).

8. Even prominent European Marxists who came here soon dropped the demand for abolition.

9. Initially "Committee for Industrial Organization," then "Congress of Industrial Organizations."

10. This point could be misleading. There were several bloody clashes between workers and local and/or state police forces— e.g., at Flint, and during the general strike in San Francisco. Here, though, Sakai is emphasizing the role of the Federal Government and the broader ruling class strategy led by Roosevelt.

11. For a version of the same history that emphasizes the CIO's commitment to organizing Black workers, see Philip Foner, op. cit., chapter 16. Foner emphasizes that after five years of the CIO's organizing (1935–1940) the number of Black trade union members rose from 100,000 to 500,000 with many trade union benefits for those workers. He admits, however, that "... such militant activities made no real dent in Negro joblessness," and that "the CIO also did little to break down the discriminatory lines in industries where blacks were employed ..." (p. 233)

12. For certain periods, immigrant Europeans were genuine workers, until they too were integrated into the settler privileged.

13. This summary of the structural crisis is taken from Christian Parenti, *Lockdown America*. Profit rate numbers can vary according to the time period selected and whether pre- or post-tax profit figures are used. The Economic Policy Institute gives the drop as from 8% to less than 5%.

14. There's a common confusion in statistics for incarceration. Prior to 1971, official numbers covered only those in state and federal prisons, while more recent figures may or may not also include those in county or city jails. Including the latter reveals numbers that are about 40% higher. Here, to be consistent, I

compare only those in prison. When we add those in jails, the U.S. incarceration rate is staggering, at above 700 per 100,000.

15. A lot more jobs were lost to productivity gains from new technologies. Traditionally, such advances generated even more jobs in other sectors of the economy. I haven't seen any definitive study on whether or not that's been happening in this period.

16. Standard "productivity" figures are skewed due to international unequal exchange and pricing. For example, the pay to the workers in the Dominican Republic who sew a garment amounts to only 1% of its final price. A lot of the higher price within the U.S. is then attributed to the "productivity" of U.S. workers. Nonetheless, these figures provide a valid comparison for showing that the levelling off of wages was not based on a decline in productivity.

17. Household wealth is another statistic that can vary according to what method is used. Here, I chose the middle figure, between 8 to 1 and 22 to 1, of the three sources I found.

18. Middle-class would include the self-employed, some professionals, and very small business people. In common U.S. usage it also includes better paid workers. That's not just an affectation. Within a global class analysis, many U.S. workers are middle-class.

Settlers: The Mythology of the White Proletariat from Mayflower to Modern

J. SAKAI • 9781629630373 • 456 PAGES • $20.00

The United States is a country built on the theft of Indigenous lands and Afrikan labor, on the robbery of the northern third of Mexico, the colonization of Puerto Rico, and the expropriation of the Asian working class, with each of these crimes being accompanied by violence. In fact, America's white citizenry have never supported themselves but have always resorted to exploitation and theft, culminating in acts of genocide to maintain their culture and way of life. This movement classic lays it all out, taking us through this painful but important history.

This new edition includes "Cash & Genocide: The True Story of Japanese-American Reparations" and an interview with author J. Sakai by Ernesto Aguilar.

Available from www.leftwingbooks.net

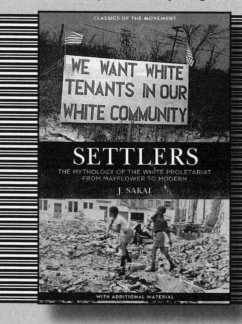

APPENDIX: Comments by J. Sakai (May 1992)

Since David Gilbert has rightfully started off a re-evaluation of the entire question of the white working class, i would like to throw a few points into the discussion. First off, i think the value of *Looking At The White Working Class Historically* is in what it attempts. Examining a class by historical materialism is something that is seldom done by revolutionaries in the u.s.

Usually class is treated in an objectified way, as a statistical category that is accepted uncritically from u.s. census reports. Which is one reason why Movement discussions of class are so ritualistic and—in truth—useless. It's when we confront a class as a living development, now and historically, that we can catch the flow of its evolution into the political future.

Gilbert puts his investigation in the right framework by moving W.E.B. DuBois's *Black Reconstruction* to the center. DuBois's massive study of what happened to that brief period of Black bourgeois democracy after the Civil War in the South—known as Black Reconstruction—was written by DuBois as a defense of his anti-integrationist views. Already being iced by the Black Elite because of his break with amerikanism, and moving toward his call for "A Negro Nation Within The Nation," DuBois aimed his history at the present. To think of *Black Reconstruction* as just about some old 19th century events is to miss DuBois's crosscourt pass.

Looking At The White Working Class Historically gets right to the question: if Class, as scientific revolutionaries believe, is the primary shaper of political consciousness, then why in amerika's 400 years has the white working class always been loyal to its capitalists (and thus its Race) not its Class? At a time when the u.s.s.r. has evaporated and national movements in the Third World are moving towards capitalism, people all over the world are rightfully questioning the value of communist ideas.

As Gilbert notes, to DuBois Black Reconstruction from 1866 to 1877 was such a telling test because it was the best chance amerika would ever have for a democratic alliance of Black & White working people. New Afrikan-led State and local governments in the ex-Confederate states lifted the poor whites up, gave *him* political rights, public education and protective labor legislation (women were, of course, excluded from this democracy). Still, the poor whites of the South remained loyal to their defeated slavemaster nation (and still cherish the "stars and bars" and "dixie" in their hearts today). As Gilbert so correctly writes:

> "In the South, the poor whites became the shock troops for the mass terror that destroyed the gains of Black Reconstruction. DuBois explains that the overthrow of Reconstruction was a property—not a Race—war. Still, the poor whites involved were not simply tools of property. They perceived their own interests in attacking the Black advances…"

In the century since Black Reconstruction the white working class has congealed, solidified, grown old actually. A white working class which has always been opposed to any real democracy is hardly a bet for Class war and revolution. Let's get real: after 400 years of waiting for the bus, this isn't even a question but a fact of life like gravity and taxes. So how does the equation end up? What's the bottom line?

Paradoxically, i believe this only proves again how "Class is everything," the primary division in the struggle between oppressor and oppressed. And the white working class is unfortunately no question at all.

Settlers is often misread to the effect that there's no white working class. Probably because it wasn't written more clearly. David Gilbert says:

> "Thus, for Sakai, there is an oppressor nation but it doesn't have a working class, at least not in any politically meaningful sense of the term … In my view, there is definitely a white working class. It is closely tied to imperialism, the labor aristocracy the dominant sector, the class as a whole has been corrupted by white supremacy; but, the class within the oppressor nation that lives by the sale of their labor power has not disappeared … under certain historical conditions it can have important meaning."

Of course, there's a white working class in amerika. *Settlers* reminds readers of Engels' point that "there are *many* working classes" (my emphasis). In world history, a great variety of working classes. The idea that there's only one kind of working class—exploited, noble, urban and industrial, male-centered, politically class-conscious—is a cardboard abstraction. That's why Walter Rodney didn't like the term, wanted to use "producers" instead. The white working class is a particular kind of working class: one that is an oppressor class, by its very nature wedded to capitalism, and not a proletariat (the proletariat is the lowest, most oppressed class in society).

A working class isn't primarily determined or shaped by the fact of working for wages. The prison warden works for a wage, after all, while the Afrikan slaves who built amerika on their backs never were wage-laborers. What is determining is the extraction of surplus value. Technically, when we say a class is exploited what we mean is that capitalism extracts surplus value (what becomes profits in the level of the marketplace) from its labor.

For example, no one can deny that there is a Boer white working class in South Africa (at least there is at this writing in 1992—this is only an example). They exist in the millions, in mines and offices and factories. They are wage laborers. Yet, as a whole, they produce no (as in zero) surplus value. Economic studies show that all the surplus value created in South Africa is created by Afrikan labor. The Boer white workers' wage labor is merely an indirect mechanism for them to share in the exploiting of Afrikans. That's why Afrikan workers live in dusty Soweto and the white working class lives in ranch-style homes with cars, appliances, .357 magnums, swimming pools and cheap Afrikan servants. They are a working class, alright, but a parasitic one with no real class consciousness and no contribution to make to the liberating of the world.

It isn't so hard to see that the same thing is true with the white working class in settler amerika (the only working classes anywhere in the world with lifestyles like the Boer workers in South Africa are those here in north amerika). David Gilbert and other white anti-imperialists certainly understand this. And as he warns: "We must guard against the mechanical notion that economic decline will in itself lessen racism ... The white workers closest to the level of Third World workers can be the most virulent and violent in fighting for white supremacy." These are apt words for the 1990s, when new reformist illusions are being spread at the same time as David Duke and racist skinheads show the renewed appeal of the white Right.

Gilbert then raises his main question of what dissenting class forces can be seen arising out of "people's relationship to the mode of production." Even privileged whites "who live by the sale of labor power" have, in Gilbert's view, different ultimate interests from "those who own or control the means of production." In amerika's future, he believes, "those who aren't in control have a basic interest in a transformation of society."

This may be true as a generalization, but what does it mean? Specifically, what is the mode of production now for white people? What is the white settler class structure really like? Without this foundation Gilbert has a seeming bind: old theory says that white wage employees (it's hard to keep calling them workers since so many don't do any work or are professionals) will be for "a transformation of society," while immediate reality tells us that for many of the poorest whites the "transformation" they want is Black Genocide.

We're trying to understand an expressway-gang-bang-ing-import-export culture of neo-colonialism with the

Class analysis and Race concepts of 100 years ago. i doubt it's true that the white working class, shrinking and ever less-important, will ever be progressive in our lifetime. Already, a class grown old, they're *backward-looking*, nostalgic, literally reactionary and recoiling from the future (like some Third World movements in amerika). I'm sorry for them, but not all that sorry.

To me, the main point is that in seeing Classes as they really are, in their historical materialist development and in their daily lives, we learn that truly change-oriented classes are new classes. Young, being born in the contradictions of social structures. Young classes that are self-consciously creating themselves as much as they are being created by anonymous social-economic forces. The young euro-bourgeoisie was once such a class: bold, adventurous, reshaping the world through a revolution in the arts and sciences as much as the cannon. In a much lesser way, for example, the impact of the new class of New Afrikan islamic male vendors, artisans and merchants today is due to a similarly bold outlook.

Naturally, i don't agree with all of David Gilbert's thoughts about the present, but appreciate how he closes *Looking At The White Working Class Historically* by connecting his examination of Class to the 1960s New Left, when some white working-class youth searching for a different way of life were stirred into joining the "Jailbreak." Although the stereotype is of student radicals from wealthy or very suburban backgrounds, a number of the most radical collectives and armed struggle groups of the 1960s were disproportionately working class in their composition. The George Jackson Brigade or the semi-underground G.I.

organizations, for instance. But then, these weren't folks trying to reform the white union at the Ajax chrome toilet factory—they wanted out of their dead culture with its racist and repressive rules and loyalties, out of their sick nation, the whole thing. They were a small minority, of course (although still many thousands, then).

When the "Ohio 7," for example, began armed action, they were a small Boston-area collective from mostly working-class backgrounds, forced underground for fighting u.s. backing of the Apartheid regime in South Africa. [Editor: see note on page 93] It would be ironic if they become the last anti-Apartheid fighters left in prison anywhere in the world.

P.S. Reading David Gilbert's *Looking At the White Working Class Historically* reminds me of C.L.R. James's insistence that "There is no Black history, there is only history." By which he meant that there is only one journey of human history and we are all in it: mixing, influencing and gate-crashing on each other's stories. Although Gilbert's paper only deals with the question of the *white* working class (and is obviously intended mainly for other white anti-imperialists) the question of Class that he pursues is just as important—and unanswered—for Third World comrades, although we've been avoiding it.

The question of Class is hardest to deal with not for

white but for Third World movements here, who have ambiguously straddled the question by embracing a unity that says we're entitled to everything the white man gets ("equality"). But no matter who lives them, those middle-class and upper working-class lifestyles (private houses, cars, appliances, credit card cultural life) come from the super-exploitation of Afrika, Asia, and Latin America. Which is why Third World movements here have both hated Amerika and have been pulled towards loving Amerika—as so many Black leaders have pointed out—"even more" than white people do.

Can you have it both ways? A revolutionary future built on us sharing the exceptional wealth from super-exploiting the Third World.

Bluntly, the oppressed world majority can't afford and doesn't need $35,000 a year civil service office workers, $50,000 a year autoworkers, or $75,000 a year computer programmers. No matter what their Race is or what continent they want to be centric about. Revolutionary change requires us to discover a new communal class culture, a different daily life.

Editors' note: The Ohio 7 were members of the United Freedom Front, an underground organization of working class people that carried out dozens of bombings of government and corporate buildings in the 1980s to protest U.S. imperialism, including American support for the apartheid regime in South Africa. The government subjected the seven—Barbara Curzi Laaman, Patricia Gros Levasseur, Jaan Laaman, Ray Luc Levasseur, Carole Manning, Tom Manning, and Richard Williams—to multiple trials on a wide range of charges stemming from their activities, including sedition and racketeering. Members of the group all had young children, and the government also unsuccessfully tried to turn to their kids into informants or threatened to hide them from their parents. Curzi, Gros, and Carole Manning were released from prison in the 1990s. Levasseur was freed in 2004. Williams was held incommunicado after 9/11, causing a heart attack; he died in prison in 2005. Jaan Laaman and Tom Manning remain in prison. For updates on their respective cases, see www.4strugglemag.org and www.thejerichomovement.com.

ACKNOWLEDGMENTS

Thank You Hearty thank-yous to Kuwasi Balagoon (deceased), Cynthia Bowman, Kathy Boudin, Bernardine Dohrn, r.n.d., Bob Feldman, Elana Levy, Claude Marks, Rob McBride, Matt Meyer, Sekou Odinga, Dave Reilly, J. Sakai, Meg Starr, Ken Yale.

An additional, very special thank you goes to Dan Berger, Naomi Jaffe, and Karl Kersplebedeb for their very consistent and prodigious help.

David Gilbert, a longtime anti-racist and anti-imperialist, first became active in the Civil Rights movement in 1961. In 1965, he started the Vietnam Committee at Columbia University; in 1967 he co-authored the first Students for a Democratic Society pamphlet naming the system "imperialism"; and he was active in the Columbia strike of 1968. He later joined the Weather Underground and spent a total of 10 years underground.

David has been imprisoned in New York State since October 20th, 1981, when a unit of the Black Liberation Army along with allied white revolutionaries tried to get funds for the struggle by robbing a Brinks truck. This tragically resulted in a shoot-out in which a Brinks guard and two police officers were killed. David is serving a sentence of 75 years (minimum) to life under New York State's "felony murder" law, whereby all participants in a robbery, even if they are unarmed and non-shooters, are equally responsible for all deaths that occur. While in prison, he's been a pioneer for peer education on AIDS and has continued to write and advocate against oppression. He's been involved with the annual Certain Days Freedom for Political Prisoners Calendar since 2001 and has written two books from prison that are available from Kersplebedeb: *No Surrender* and *Love and Struggle*, as well as the pamphlet *Our Commitment is to Our Communities: Mass Incarceration, Political Prisoners and Building a Movement for Community-Based Justice*.

As of this printing (October 2017), you can write to David at:

David Gilbert #83A6158
Wende Correctional Facility,
3040 Wende Road
Alden, New York 14004-1187

RECOMMENDED

No Surrender:
Writings from an
Anti-Imperialist
Political Prisoner

DAVID GILBERT

Published in 2004 by AG PRESS

9781894925266 • 283 PAGES • $15.00

This first collection of David Gilbert's
prison writings is a unique contribution
to our understanding of the most
ambitious and audacious attempts
by white anti-imperialists to build an
underground movement "within the
belly of the beast." With unsparing
honesty (and unfailing humor), he
discusses the errors and successes of the
Weather Underground and its allies;
the pitfalls of racism, sexism, and ego
in revolutionary organizations; and the
possibilities and perils facing today's
growing anti-imperialist resistance.
Includes forewords by political
prisoners Marilyn Buck (rest in power)
and Sundiata Acoli.

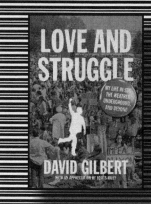

Love and Struggle:
My Life in SDS, the
Weather Underground,
and Beyond

DAVID GILBERT

Published in 2011 by PM PRESS

9781604863192 • 336 PAGES
$22.00

Today a beloved and
admired mentor to a new
generation of activists, in this
autobiography David Gilbert
assesses with rare humor,
with an understanding
stripped of illusions, and
with uncommon candor
the errors and advances,
terrors and triumphs of the
Sixties and beyond. With an
introduction by Boots Riley.

READINGS

Our Commitment is to Our Communities

DAVID GILBERT • 9781894946650
34 PAGES • $5.00

In this pamphlet, interviewed by Bob Feldman, political prisoner David Gilbert discusses the ongoing catastrophe that is mass incarceration, connecting it to the continued imprisonment of political prisoners and the challenges that face our movements today.

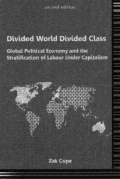

Divided World Divided Class: Global Political Economy and the Stratification of Labour Under Capitalism

ZAK COPE • 9781894946681
460 PAGES • $24.95

Charting the history of the "labour aristocracy" in the capitalist world system, from its roots in colonialism to its birth and eventual maturation into a full-fledged middle class in the age of imperialism. Demonstrating not only how redistribution of income derived from super-exploitation has allowed for the amelioration of class conflict in the wealthy capitalist countries, but also that the exorbitant "super-wage" paid to workers there has meant the disappearance of a domestic vehicle for socialism, an exploited working class. Rather, in its place is a deeply conservative metropolitan workforce committed to maintaining, and even extending, its privileged position through imperialism.

AVAILABLE FROM KERSPLEBEDEB /// ORDER FROM LEFTWINGBOOKS.NET

The Worker Elite: Notes on the "Labor Aristocracy"

BROMMA
9781894946575
88 PAGES • $10.00

Revolutionaries often say that the working class holds the key to overthrowing capitalism. But "working class" is a very broad category—so broad that it can be used to justify a whole range of political agendas. *The Worker Elite: Notes on the "Labor Aristocracy"* breaks it all down, criticizing opportunists who minimize the role of privilege within the working class, while also challenging simplistic Third Worldist analyses.

Jailbreak Out of History: the Re-Biography of Harriet Tubman

BUTCH LEE • 9781894946704
169 PAGES • $14.95

Anticolonial struggles of New Afrikan/ Black women were central to the unfolding of 19th century amerika, both during and "after" slavery. "The Re-Biography of Harriet Tubman" recounts the life and politics of Harriet Tubman, who waged and eventually lead the war against the capitalist slave system. A second text in this second edition volume, "The Evil of Female Loaferism," details New Afrikan women's attempts to withdraw from and evade capitalist colonialism, an unofficial but massive labor strike which threw the capitalists North and South into a panic. The ruling class response consisted of the "Black Codes," Jim Crow, re-enslavement through prison labor, mass violence, and … the establishment of a neo-colonial Black patriarchy, whose task was to make New Afrikan women subordinate to New Afrikan men, just as New Afrika was supposed to be subordinate to white amerika.

Amazon Nation or Aryan Nation: White Women and the Coming of Black Genocide

BOTTOMFISH BLUES • 9781894946551
168 PAGES • $12.95

Raw and vital lessons at the violent crash scene of nation, gender, and class, from a revolutionary perspective. The two main essays in this book come from the radical women's newspaper *Bottomfish Blues* in the late 1980s and early '90s; while a historical appendix on "The Ideas of Black Genocide in the Amerikkkan Mind" was written more recently, but only circulated privately.

Exodus And Reconstruction: Working-Class Women at the Heart of Globalization

BROMMA • 9781894946421 • 37 PAGES. • $3.00

In this pamphlet Bromma examines the decline of traditional rural patriarchy under neocolonial globalization, and the position of women at the heart of a transformed global proletariat.

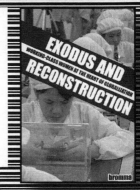

Eurocentrism and the Communist Movement

ROBERT BIEL • 9781894946711 • 215 PAGES • $17.95

Looking at Eurocentrism, alienation, and racism, tracing different ideas about imperialism, colonialism, "progress," and non-European peoples, as they have been grappled with by revolutionaries in both the colonized and colonizing nations over the past 150 years.

the "DANGEROUS CLASS" and REVOLUTIONARY THEORY

thoughts on the making of the lumpen/proletariat

J. Sakai

The "Dangerous Class" and Revolutionary Theory: Thoughts on the Making of the Lumpen/Proletariat + Mao Z's Revolutionary Laboratory & The Lumpen/Proletariat

J. SAKAI • 9781894946902 • 308 PAGES • $24.95

From the day Marx & Engels' Communist Manifesto first lit up the "dangerous class" of jumbled criminals and outcasts on the far margins of society—those stickup-boys and sex workers and thieves and mercenaries whom they named the lumpen/proletariat—radicals have been uncertain what their role should be, and even how they should be discussed.

J. Sakai plunges in headfirst, examining the birth of the modern lumpen/ proletariat in the 18th and 19th centuries, and the storm cloud of revolutionary theory that surrounded them, going back and piecing together both the actual social reality and the analyses primarily of Marx but also Bakunin and Engels.

The second paper takes over on the flip side of the book; examining how the class analysis finally used by Mao Z was shaken out of the shipping crate from Europe and then modified to map the organizing of millions over a prolonged generational revolutionary war. One could hardly wish for a larger test tube, and the many lessons to be learned from this mass political experience are finally put on the table.

The Certain Days calendar is a joint fundraising and educational project between outside organizers in Montreal and Toronto, and three political prisoners being held in maximum-security prisons in New York State: David Gilbert, Robert Seth Hayes and Herman Bell. As the collective explains, "The initial project was suggested by Herman, and has been shaped throughout the process by all of our ideas, discussions, and analysis. All of the members of the outside collective are involved in day-to-day organizing work other than the calendar, on issues ranging from refugee and immigrant solidarity to community media to prisoner justice. We work from an anti-imperialist, anti-racist, anti-capitalist, feminist, queer and trans positive position."

Certain Days
c/o QPIRG Concordia
1455 de Maisonneuve Blvd. O.
Montreal, QC H3G 1M8
CANADA
email: info@certaindays.org
web: www.certaindays.org

to place an order:
www.leftwingbooks.net/certaindays

KER SPL EBE DEB

Since 1998 Kersplebedeb has been an important source of radical literature and agit prop materials.

The project has a non-exclusive focus on anti-patriarchal and anti-imperialist politics, framed within an anticapitalist perspective. A special priority is given the continuing struggles of political prisoners and prisoners of war.

The Kersplebedeb website presents historical and contemporary writings by revolutionary thinkers from the anarchist and communist traditions. At the same time, the leftwingbooks.net website serves as Kersplebedeb's storefront, with well over a thousand progressive books and pamphlets available for mail-order.

Kersplebedeb can be contacted at:

Kersplebedeb
CP 63560
CCCP Van Horne
Montreal, Quebec
Canada
H3W 3H8

email: info@kersplebedeb.com
web: www.kersplebedeb.com
           www.leftwingbooks.net

Kersplebedeb